HONG KONG IN ITS REGIONAL SETTING

Series AR/18/IRS
Edition 1   1996

Cartography by Survey and Mapping Office, Lands Department
© Copyright reserved — reproduction by permission only

LEGEND

— / - - -	Railway / under construction
— / - - -	Main road / under construction
—	Secondary road
∎∎∎∎♦	Special Economic Zone Boundary
▨ / ▨	Built-up area / Cultivation
• Changping	Town
✈ / ⚡	Airport / Power station
▲ 869	Contours / Peak (in metres) (vertical interval 200 metres with supplementary contour at 100 metres)
	Sea depth in metres

MW01596338

Markets at Work

Dynamics of the Residential Real Estate Market in Hong Kong

Markets at Work
Dynamics of the Residential Real Estate Market in Hong Kong

B. Renaud, F. Pretorius and B. Pasadilla

Hong Kong University Press
香港大學出版社

Hong Kong University Press
The University of Hong Kong
Pokfulam Road, Hong Kong

© Hong Kong University Press 1997

ISBN 962 209 438 4

All rights reserved. No portion of this publication may
be reproduced or transmitted in any form or by any recording,
or any information storage or retrieval system, without permission
in writing from the publisher.

The maps reproduced with the permission of The Director of Lands,
© Hong Kong Government Licence No. 20/1997.

The publication of this book is made possible with support by the
Centre for Real Estate and Urban Economics, which is associated with the
Department of Real Estate and Construction at the University of Hong Kong. The
primary task of the Centre is to examine issues relevant to the real estate community's
investment programmes in Hong Kong, China and elsewhere in the region.

Printed in Hong Kong by ColorPrint Production Co. Ltd.

CONTENTS

ILLUSTRATIONS

Figures

TABLES

PREFACE

The real estate economy of Hong Kong is one of the most dynamic and sophisticated in the world. Perhaps more importantly, at a time of rapid globalization of the world economy, it is possibly the best model that exists in the world of the behaviour of an advanced real estate industry operating in an open economy. There is therefore considerable international interest in the features that have made Hong Kong's real estate economy so flexible and responsive to changing domestic and international conditions. This interest comes from international real estate professionals who would like to know how Hong Kong's investment and financing techniques compare with other advanced economies. It also comes from policymakers and regulators who want to understand better the key legal, institutional and regulatory features which have permitted this major sector to become increasingly flexible, sophisticated and efficient over the last fifty years. Economists active in international development agencies and others who are interested in comparative analysis of economic institutions also have had a long-standing interest in all aspects of the Asian Tiger economies of which Hong Kong is possibly the most interesting example.

We do not believe that there is an urgent need for a comprehensive textbook on the real estate industry in Hong Kong, nor would there be much value in a purely descriptive book; solid factual descriptions of the sector in Hong Kong already exist. The problem is also not one of raw information: in Hong Kong, reliable real estate information is abundant compared to most countries. Therefore, looking beyond 1997 at the impact of globalization on the real estate sector, the objective of this book is to highlight the *key factors* which shape the *dynamics* of the Hong Kong real estate industry. In order to achieve this objective and maximize its comparative value, we conduct an analysis of the private residential market in Hong Kong, using the Fisher-DiPasquale-Wheaton theoretical model of a real estate economy. This theoretical representation of the industry is rapidly becoming the standard paradigm for the analysis of a real estate economy, and enables us to identify and concentrate our analysis on the most critical features which shape the dynamics of the Hong Kong real estate markets, and their interactions with domestic and international capital markets. The present test shows that the FDW model is an excellent vehicle for organizing efficiently the complex baseline required to understand the dynamics of a given real estate market, and for identifying and analysing the implications of policy initiatives on the sector.

The approach that we use throughout the book is to provide accessible insights into the dynamics of the Hong Kong real estate economy, drawing on limited but appropriate technical analysis and historical resources. In developing insights into the nature of the industry, we used time-series data generally covering the period 1980–1995, but it will soon become clear to readers that the relationships identified are useful in scenario projections and event analyses independent of this time frame. Our goal will have been reached if the book enables an experienced specialist who is new to Hong Kong to arrive quickly at a correct understanding of this key industry before investigating in more depth some individual aspect of the industry. We hope that this concise (re)interpretation of the residential real estate sector in Hong Kong will be of value to international and Hong Kong analysts and decision makers.

We are particularly pleased to offer this monograph as the inaugural publication of the Centre for Real Estate and Urban Economics, associated with the Department of Real Estate and Construction at the University of Hong Kong. We also gratefully acknowledge funding for the project from the Committee for Research and Conference Grants at the University of Hong Kong. We are, of course, responsible for errors.

Bertrand M. Renaud
Frederik Pretorius
Bernabe O. Pasadilla

Centre for Real Estate and Urban Economics
The University of Hong Kong
April 1997

Plate 1 Modern Residential Real Estate in Hong Kong
Modern, luxurious and in an expensive and fashionable location — but density and high-rise
characteristics prevail.

Plate 2

Plate 3

Plates 2 and 3 Hong Kong: High Density, High-Rise Urban Development
This is an illustration of Hong Kong's response over the years to limited land supply and severe topographical constraints: high-density, high-rise urban development with intensive and mixed use of land. Given the constraints on land resources, competition for land among industrial, commercial, residential, environmental, recreational and infrastructure uses, and between personal and freight movement is among the most severe in Asian cities.

1 INTRODUCTION

The real estate sector forms a major part of any economy both by its sheer size and also by its extensive influence on the various sectors of the economy. With its various components, it has the unique characteristics of being simultaneously a major input in the productive capacity of the economy in the case of office, commercial and industrial real estate and a major input in the consumption choices of households in the case of residential real estate. It is also an important investment vehicle for both individual and institutional investors as an investment good, while also being the output of the development and construction industry and as such also a major consumer of manufacturers output. In many cases it forms the principal form of saving for many households. These factors ensure that the performance of the real estate sector in any well-functioning market economy remains a closely watched phenomenon — in Hong Kong perhaps more so than in many other economies.

Despite the importance of the real estate sector to economies generally, economists have been slow to develop useful tools to conduct analyses of the sector, and to some extent this reflects in the forms of analysis still widely used in many markets. Typically real estate markets are viewed as bounded by the limits of particular cities or larger urban concentrations (for example, the Hong Kong metropolitan area would be an appropriate unit of analysis if industrial real estate was the object of analysis); or on the other hand cities were broken down into smaller units of analysis — 'submarkets' (for example, within Hong Kong's retail sector Causeway Bay could be viewed as a distinct submarket). Such approaches generally suit the immediate information requirements and activities of real estate professionals active in the valuation, letting and selling of property, and allowed some market analyses based on data so aggregated. But typically such analyses also remain fragmented, and of course, the amount of information so put into the public domain remains dictated by the commercial interests of those conducting the analyses — it does not generally make much commercial sense for a real estate developer to disclose the results of an in-depth market analysis of a particular sector or a particular location. It may also not make sense for consultants who advise investors to make all their proprietary information public. These considerations contribute to making the business of real estate highly information-intensive and sensitive to detail at the level where actual transactions are conducted, and ensures to some extent that a substitute for in-depth local market knowledge is remote if not impossible.

There are further shortcomings in traditional approaches to the analysis of real estate markets. The institutions and structural characteristics that make particular markets function well or poorly (or perhaps not at all) are themselves very seldom the focus of analysis, despite the importance of these institutions and structures in the allocation of an extremely important resource in urban-based economics — the scarce resource land. The efficiency of the institutions and practices associated with the management of land is becoming an increasingly important matter with continuing urbanization in many countries worldwide. For these and other reasons that will become clear in this book, the institutions and practices put in place to manage land as a scarce economic resource in Hong Kong are of critical interest to policymakers everywhere, including those in the People's Republic of China and other Asian countries with high-density urban development.

The Demand for International Comparative Analysis from Market Participants and Policymakers

As much of the actual commerce of the real estate industry in all economies remains to be conducted at a local level, it can easily be considered the only level that matters critically when real estate markets are analysed — this characterization is naturally a mistake. Local market transactions may be dominated by local participants (either as agents or as principals), but at least two recent crucial international developments demand that detailed local information be supplemented by analyses of the structure and dynamics of real estate sectors beyond analyses of market demand and supply trends. As is often the case with such things, these two phenomena have not been entirely separable and have had individual and combined influence on the conduct of business in real estate markets everywhere. We mention and briefly describe these two phenomena hereunder, because they form an important underlying reason for the demand from real estate economists for analyses of the sort that form the subject of this book. To some extent, these demands have preceded demands for comparative analyses from policymakers.

What were these large-scale trends? They both have to do with the worldwide institutionalization of all investment activities, including investment in securitized real estate and also direct investment in particularly commercial real estate assets.

The first international development is now a largely historical fact, and can be described as the domination of financial institutions (i.e. pension funds, insurance companies, etc.) of investment activities in most advanced market economies in all forms of investment goods, including stocks, bonds, derivatives, etc.; and which also spawned the parallel growth and maturity of funds management as an industry over the last two to three decades. Hong Kong is indeed a centre from where fund management activities in all major world markets are transacted.

In Hong Kong, institutional investors, either directly or through fund managers, have not been as active in real estate markets as elsewhere, in some measure as a consequence of the absence of securitized investment vehicles such as real estate investment trusts and other real estate investment vehicles that exist elsewhere (with the exception of a small number of mortgage-backed securities);[1] but it could also be argued that the high incidence of owner-occupation of real estate in Hong Kong and small asset size (and high prices) have mitigated against it. Elsewhere, the institutional influence has greatly increased the demands on real estate investment analysts — investment analysis techniques moved rapidly beyond discounted cash flow (a staple of the 1960s and early 1970s) as a fundamental technique for analysing any investment (including real estate), towards the formal tools of modern portfolio theory which demands a formal treatment of the combination of all investment goods (including real estate assets) within a risk/return asset allocation framework. Therefore, the first international trend started to break down the highly local nature of real estate investment analysis practices, and culminated in the demand by institutional portfolio investors and fund managers for more formal techniques of investment analysis to inform real estate investment decision-making. Direct and other forms of institutional investment activities will increase in Hong Kong real estate with inevitable legislative liberation of institutional investment activities and further development of the financial sector; and associated therewith the inevitable insistence on investment analyses aimed at supporting the construction of optimum investment portfolios are likely to become the standard as has happened elsewhere.

At the same time as separate market economies were standardizing investment analysis techniques as a consequence of the demand and influence of institutional portfolio investors, the second development was quietly gathering momentum: this is the globalization of the world economy generally, and more specifically for our purposes, the international mobility of capital. With the rapid globalization of financial markets, institutional investors extended not only their attempts to optimize the allocation of their investments generally, but also their investment in real estate in both domestic and international markets. Large corporations operating across countries also have to meet their real estate needs in global markets, as witnessed by the rapidly growing field of corporate real estate management. Together with the international mobility of direct investment capital and investment portfolio capital, and therewith the international activities of institutional investors, there were thus created further demands on real estate professionals functioning in local markets from institutions that were considering investment in direct and/or securitized real estate investment in those markets. Predictably, there arose a demand for reliable comparative analyses of real estate markets and institutions across countries, regions and even between sectors in local markets.

The demand for analytical information over the last two decades were, however, not limited to potential investors; the demand by policymakers and regulators has also been growing rapidly. Powerful interactions between real estate and macroeconomic management decisions during the 1985–1994 real estate cycle have demonstrated the need to understand better the impact of real estate asset inflation on monetary and exchange rate policies in Japan, the UK and the Nordic countries (Renaud, 1997). Bank failures are also too regularly associated with real estate cycles (witness the instability in the Hong Kong financial system during the period 1983–86, the US Savings and Loan crisis of 1989–93, and the present instability in the Japanese financial system). Furthermore, increasing competition between cities in a rapidly globalizing economy has highlighted the importance of land resources and their management to local enonomies, and the benefits to be gained from efficient use of scarce land resources. All too often this requirement is coupled with intense pressure from rapidly urbanizing populations, which create additional and severe pressure on the structure of demand for land use and allocation of the resource.

The demand for comparative analyses of real estate markets required at least some internationally accepted analytical framework for it to be viewed as reliable and useful. But unlike an existing and ready suite of analytical techniques in financial economics that could be adopted and adapted for real estate investment, no formal economics frameworks existed or had been developed to allow for such international comparative analyses of real estate markets and institutions. The problem for comparative work of real estate markets, therefore, is that the real estate sector seems to be the last major economic sector of the economy for which international standards of evaluation are being developed. Trade, industry, agriculture, services, labour markets have generally agreed standards of evaluation — or at least much better ones than real estate.

The demand for an internationally acceptable, rigorous framework for comparative analyses of real estate markets and institutions has resulted in a sustained effort by economists to develop models to conduct and present the result of analyses of real estate markets in ways that are appropriate to those with global concerns. In a study of the private residential real estate market in Hong Kong, this book explores the use of such a model, one that could be described as the 'modern paradigm of the real estate economy' — an elegant integrated model of the real estate economy developed by Jeffrey Fisher and later completed by Denise DiPasquale and William

Wheaton (Fisher, 1992; DiPasquale and Wheaton, 1992). Use of the model forces analysts to consider a range of important structural and dynamic factors in their analysis of a particular real estate market, in order to compare such factors across markets usefully and reliably. Although the model has gained widespread acceptance in academic circles, a body of work is still required to test its usefulness in practice. We attempt such a test in this book — in essence we are attempting to answer a number of questions about the model: can it be used effectively to present the interactive features of the wider economy and of the endogenous characteristics of the real estate sector that explains its dynamics? Is it a good vehicle for reporting in a systematic way the key economic, institutional, financial and regulatory features that must be known to understand the dynamics of a given market for these to be of any use for international comparisons? Can we move away from international comparisons that are typically partial, fragmented, and too often anecdotal or frequently simplistic trend analyses by using this model? We therefore present this book as a test of the organizing powers of the FDW model for Hong Kong, and hope that it would provide a benchmark of sorts as the first test of its kind of a Hong Kong real estate market segment (and to our knowledge the first in Asia).

Why Hong Kong?

We offer two main reasons for choosing the Hong Kong real estate economy to test the FDW model as an expository framework and analytical tool, although intuitively there are certainly many more. First, Hong Kong has one of the most dynamic and sophisticated real estate economies in the world. Perhaps more importantly, at a time of rapid globalization of the world economy, Hong Kong is possibly the best model that exists anywhere of the behaviour of an advanced real estate industry operating in an open economy. There is, therefore, widespread international interest in identifying and presenting introductory analyses of the specific institutions and regulatory features that have made Hong Kong's real estate economy so flexible and responsive to changing domestic and international conditions.

The analyses presented in the rest of this book indeed identifies regulatory and structural features that have served this community exceptionally well in the allocation of scarce land resources. We think of the highly flexible people of Hong Kong which have dramatically restructured their economy within two decades — flexibility that has never been witnessed elsewhere (Chapter 2). We think of rapidly and efficiently changing real estate rental and asset prices, mostly unrestricted by arbitrary controls and political interference but subject to independent financial regulatory discipline within an open economy (Chapters 3 and 4). We further think of the extremely efficient delivery mechanisms of the major real estate developers in Hong Kong, and the extreme constraints that restrictions on the supply of developable land places on the community (Chapter 5); a constraint that is clearly placing limitations on preferred patterns of consumption of real estate services in the city (Chapter 6).

Our second reason for presenting this analysis is the hope that identification of those factors that have contributed to the spectacular performance of the real estate sector in Hong Kong will urge caution upon policymakers in future when considering policy towards the sector. It is a fact that inappropriate interventions are a permanent threat to well functioning real estate markets everywhere, because real estate assets are the longest lived investments in the economy along with investment in physical infrastructure. We therefore hope hereby to emphasize the importance of factors and institutions which contributed to success, and possibly contribute insights into factors that have proven to be constraints on the residential real estate market in Hong Kong.

The Modern Real Estate Paradigm and the Fisher-DiPasquale-Wheaton Model

In order to introduce the nature of the relationships represented by the Fisher-DiPasquale-Wheaton (FDW) model and how these help to provide insights into the functioning of real estate economies, we ask the reader to indulge first in the statement of a limited number of simple but fundamental economic concepts that apply to most capital goods (or producer goods including real estate) in an economy. We divide these concepts into four, which in turn we choose to label the four 'building blocks' of the FDW model. The concept of economic depreciation is introduced first because it perhaps requires the most detailed explanation and concepts to explain the remaining three.

At a fundamental level, most capital goods in an economy, such as machine tools, are used in the various intermediate stages of producing a product or service for which there has to be a final end-user demand — a 'derived demand' (a frequently encountered concept in real estate economics textbooks). Useful examples of capital goods applicable to the analyses that follow are freight ships, container ships or bulk cargo carriers, freight aircraft, trucks and other motor vehicles (including vehicles such as passenger cars that may be used either as a capital good in a production process, or as privately owned transportation). This categorization includes real estate assets. Central to the understanding of the economics of all such capital goods is that there is an aggregate demand in the economy for the function provided by the capital good. For example, there is at any time an aggregate demand for air freight services in an economy, measured perhaps as an annual, monthly, weekly, or even daily tonnage that customers require to have moved on a particular route.

Typically, this aggregate demand is satisfied by a stock of capital goods that exist in the economy, and this total stock (or aggregate supply) will produce the required amount of output of services per period — the 'flow' of products or services demanded and thus supplied. If we continue the air freight example, this flow of demand will determine the overall aggregate supply capacity of the stock of capital goods producing the flow of goods. In the air freight example, this will be the total number of aircraft required to service the flow of demand, and will be influenced by factors such as asset cost, travel time on the route, aircraft turnaround time, and other constraints particular to that industry. As long as there is no change in the flow of demand (i.e. no expansion or contraction), or as long as there is no change in the capacity of the stock to produce the required service, there will be no reason to increase the number of assets in the total stock. We have thus an equilibrium position.

However, capital goods wear out (*economic depreciation*) and have to be replaced. (For example, an aircraft eventually becomes dangerous or too costly to maintain and has to be replaced; office buildings have to be renovated or redeveloped.) Alternatively, technological advances and innovation introduce improvements which render older stock uncompetitive despite long economic lives. (For example, a new aircraft produces the same service as an old one at a substantially reduced operating cost.) Under both these conditions and despite static demand, there will thus be a demand for the replacement of depreciated or uneconomical capital goods, including also real estate assets as a class of capital good. This 'replacement demand' for depreciated assets is a fundamental factor in all sectors of the economy that produce capital goods as a business activity, including real estate developers and construction companies. This concept forms an important building block of the FDW model and will be returned to in the rest of the book.

We commenced the discussion by assuming that the aggregate demand for the services produced by the stock of capital goods is static — leading to the conclusion that demand for new assets is thereby restricted to the *replacement demand* for depreciated assets. If aggregate demand expands, however, there will be a demand for additional units of the capital good — and the aggregate stock will expand to meet the higher aggregate demand. In turn, with an increased stock this should cause an increase in the absolute replacement demand from economic depreciation, even though the *rate of depreciation* of the capital good may not change. So the industries that produce or build the capital good changes capacity first in line with demand to expand the stock, and thereafter changes capacity again to service an increased replacement demand from depreciation. Of course, when aggregate demand reduces, the process is reversed.

We can now rapidly introduce the remaining three building blocks of the FDW model. There will not be a demand for new capital assets if their function was not valued — i.e. if the price for their output of goods or services was not economical, or the benefit gained from owning them did not exceed the cost. We are then further concerned with three concepts that have to do with prices surrounding the capital good, and these three concepts underlie the remaining building blocks of the FDW model. The next building block is the price that a user of the capital good will pay to secure the right to use the asset, i.e. the *market price* for use of the asset given the *aggregate demand and stock of capital goods*. To the owner of the aircraft, from our earlier example, this is represented by the unit price that can be earned for carrying air freight on the route in question, or for the owner of a commercial property this is the market rent paid by a tenant to use the property. In the case of some capital goods this is not always an absolutely clearly identifiable cash consideration, as could be the case for example with capital goods that produce a stream of services in private household consumption use such as privately-owned cars or privately-owned residential properties. The price for the good or service generated by the capital asset is then the second building block of the FDW model.

The next concept surrounding prices and the capital good is the *price of the capital asset* itself, which must clearly be related to the market price of its services at a time, but it is also related to how long it can generate a flow of services, so the rate at which the asset depreciates is relevant. The asset has an economic life and the revenue to the owner generated by the sale of services flowing from the asset over its economic life is therefore viewed as the principal determinant of the asset's value; but it is also possible that future revenue is uncertain — expected changes in future revenue (growth, or even decline) are important. expectation therefore play an important role in considerations of what an asset's value is, and different expectation are to be expected. Alternatively, if the prospective buyer intends to hold the asset for a shorter period than its economic life, it introduces the market for second-hand assets into the analysis (the secondary market).

The accepted methodology to estimate a value from an expected future revenue stream over a holding period is the discounted cash flow method. However, the riskiness of the revenue stream generated by the asset is also important, because there may be other investment opportunities which may generate the same revenue with less risk and would thus be preferable. If we separate for the purposes of explanation investments in capital goods from the rights to their use and revenue from their use, we see that investors in capital goods for their economic returns have a wide choice of investments — direct investment in the capital good itself (a machine tool; a car; an aircraft; a commercial, industrial or residential property), or a range of indirect forms of investment (such as through securities markets). Investors choose which capital assets to purchase based on competing returns, so competition from alternative capital assets affects the relative demand for all forms of capital investment. Competing returns is the principle underlying the economic concept of opportunity cost. The third building block of the FDW model thus encompasses the processes whereby asset prices are determined and incorporates the principles of comparable returns and risk from investment opportunities in alternative capital assets.

The fourth building block is perhaps the least complex, and draws on the outcome of asset pricing principles discussed above. It also requires further reference to the rate at which particular capital assets depreciate. Recall that we stated that when aggregate demand for products and services generated by the stock of capital assets was static, the demand for new assets would be a function of the rate at which the existing stock of assets depreciates. The *supply of new assets*, however, is constrained by the cost of producing new assets (and therefore also by the cost of the inputs required to make or build the new assets). Furthermore, if new assets cannot be produced at a lower cost than the price investors are willing to pay for them, then they will clearly not be supplied irrespective of the rate of depreciation. Supply of new assets at a profit is therefore a requirement to satisfy demand for new assets, and forms the fourth building block of the FDW model.

We have so far introduced the economic principles underlying the FDW model as these apply to capital goods in general. The formalized FDW model integrates all these concepts into one multi-directional framework that shows the relationships between common variables in different processes. In the following chapters, relevant aspects of the model and the dynamics surrounding the relationships embodied in the model will be elaborated upon. The FDW model views the real estate economy as a system in equilibrium, summarized by four quadrants divided vertically into the space market on the right and the investment or capital market on the left (as shown in Figure 1.1).

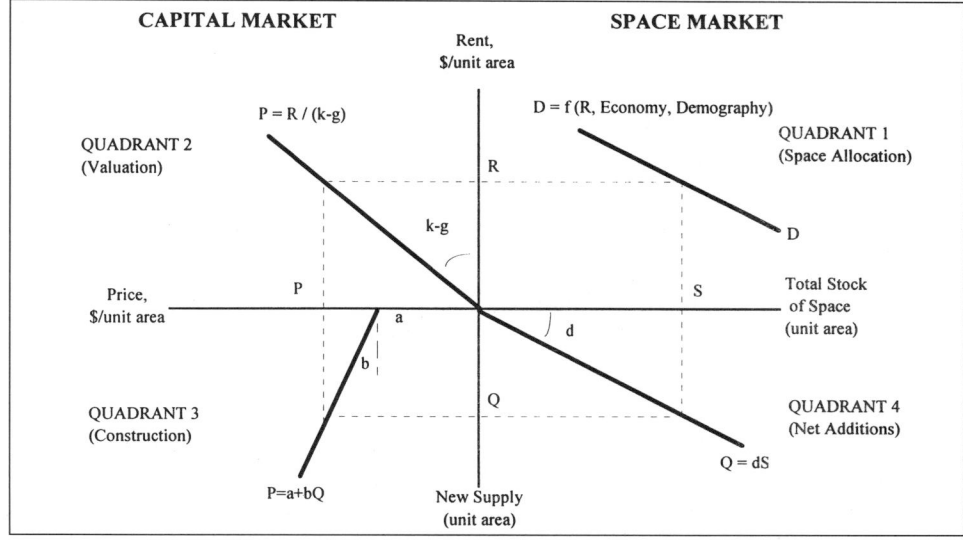

Source: Following DiPasquale and Wheaton, 1996.

Figure 1.1   Two-Sector, Four-Quadrant Model of the Real Estate Economy

The model is read counter-clockwise from the upper-right quadrant. The fundamental principle underlying the model is that the dynamics of the real estate market starts with the determination of the level of net rental income **R** at a particular time (the price for the service produced by the asset) represented here in *Quadrant 1*. In a given period, the rental income that a real estate asset commands per unit area depends on the demand for and the availability of existing space. When demand is stable and the market clears the rent level will be **R**. Curve **D** illustrates a typical demand curve for the use of space offered by real estate assets. With an ability to pay higher rents, perhaps through increased corporate earnings, the curve **D** would tend to shift upwards and with static supply this would result in higher rents. Similarly, if there was an aggregate increase in demand, curve **D** would shift to the right; also with resultant higher rents should supply remain static. The level of rent earned by real estate assets directly effects their attractiveness as investment goods and therefore the process of asset price formation in the market for real estate investment. We know that the level of rents is determined in the space market, but also that rental income is a prime consideration in asset pricing. Investors purchase a current and future rental income stream, and the observed prices reflect the current valuation of the expected rental income stream (DiPasquale and Wheaton, 1992). expectation of risk adjusted returns on alternative investments in the capital markets determine the relative attraction of real estate assets over other capital assets (*Quadrant 2*). For a given level of interest rate and required rate of return, **k**, the rent level **R** leads to a present value (or market price) **P** per unit area derived from the rental income stream generated by the asset, while also considering the expected growth, **g**, in rental income. A comparable process determines **P** for owner-occupation of real estate assets. This valuation level **P** in turn triggers decisions to develop new real estate assets by the development and construction industry.

The supply process forms the second half of the real estate investment process (*Quadrant 3*). New development projects result from entrepreneurial decisions about possible net margins to be earned on developing new real estate for sale, given the current market price of new assets, the costs of all inputs and then also the organization, structure and performance of the industry. Quadrant 3 therefore presents a standard supply schedule for the development industry, i.e. the basic environment where decisions are made to supply new real estate. Such new construction represents only gross additions to the stock. Based on the rate at which real estate assets depreciate and become obsolete, part of the existing supply will be removed from the market. *Quadrant 4* represents the process of adjustment in the total stock of real estate assets, i.e. the replacement of fully depreciated and/or functionally obsolete assets over time. This completes the second part of the space market and so closes the model. Under stable demand for real estate services with a stable rent level **R** and no price changes, the amount of new stock developed would only replace the stock withdrawn because of economic obsolescence or physical depreciation from use over time. The net adjustment to the total stock would be zero as long as there are no expansions or contractions in demand. Then there will also be no adjustments in net rental levels.

The FDW model of the modern real estate paradigm is therefore an efficient and elegant way of representing on a single page all the complex factors that shape real estate cycles. An important point to emphasize at this stage is that the FDW model is an equilibrium model — it presents a static view of the concepts discussed above and does not attempt to identify the process whereby adjustment takes place from one equilibrium position to the next. This adjustment process is dynamic and will vary in different markets, across different land uses and in different economies. The model can represent every segment of the real estate market: residential, commercial or retail, offices and industrial real estate. It forms a framework to identify and discuss the dynamics of the relationships within all sectors prior to in-depth empirical analysis of such dynamics. Once completed for the particular real estate sector under analysis, the model can be used for initial qualitative evaluation of various questions such as new policies towards the real estate sector or anticipated structural or cyclical changes in the wider economy; thus perhaps leading to the identification of critical factors that may otherwise be overlooked.

Is Private Residential Real Estate Representative of the Overall Hong Kong Real Estate Industry Dynamics?

We chose the private residential real estate sector in Hong Kong as subject of analysis for the book, with immediate appreciation of the fact that different sectors of the markets (commercial, industrial) do have different dynamic characteristics. However, we also believe that all sectors of the real estate industry in Hong Kong have important characteristics in common, which in our opinion makes the private residential sector a reasonable proxy for the behaviour of other sectors and the market as a whole. Common characteristics of all sectors include the following:

*   All sectors exhibit an extremely fragmented asset ownership pattern facilitated by very well-developed and accepted strata-title legislation. There also exists high rates of owner-occupation in all sectors including the office, retail, industrial and industrial/office sectors.
*   Short term leases, high rates of mobility and very efficient and rapid rental price adjustments characterize all sectors.
*   Price sensitivity of tenants is high and frequent relocation is not uncommon.
*   Barriers to entry for developers into all sectors are high and are increasingly so. All sectors face similar factor constraints, namely individual access to land, capital

requirements, and higher redevelopment costs than in greenfield projects of yesteryears; while delivery methods for all sectors use similar high rise building technology and are subject to the same project scale economies.

- Significant lead times between decisions to invest and unit deliveries apply in all sectors. However, it has to be pointed out that Hong Kong lead times are possibly short when compared to development activities of comparable scale and complexity in other economies.

- Rapid real estate asset price adjustments occur in all sectors.

- Close links exist between capital market conditions and sector pricing behaviour.

Table 1.1 presents some descriptive statistics of the total stock of residential real estate in Hong Kong.

From these statistics we see that in 1995 approximately 49.1% of the housing stock is public housing (853 000 units). Approximately 50.9% (885 700 units) of housing units are privately owned with approximately 75% owner-occupied. The private stock is classified into five categories by size, namely *Class A* (smaller than 40 m²), *Class B* (40–70 m²), *Class C* (70–100 m²), *Class D* (100–160 m²) and *Class E* (larger than 160 m²). We categorize Class A, B and C collectively as small units, and Class D and E as large (or luxury) units. As small- and medium-sized units form the bulk (92.6%) of the overall private housing stock and is of greatest interest to market participants in Hong Kong, we generally concentrate our analysis on this combined category.

A glaring feature of the statistics in Table 1.1 is the very large proportion (49.1% in 1995) of public housing in the total stock. We immediately agree that it would be incorrect to proceed without recognizing that this is a serious anomaly in Hong Kong's housing sector brought about by the large proportion of public housing, but in our view it adds to this test of the internal consistency of the FDW model. It must also be pointed out that this is a conspicuous exception to the Hong Kong principle that the public sector provides the regulatory environment and the private market takes care of supply based on market factors only. Housing is the single sector of the Hong Kong economy where the government has intervened massively, initially by historical accident rather than by design following the great Shek Kip Mei fire of Christmas Day 1953. This role which started fortuitously in 1953 has steadily expanded over time and presently it can be argued that the public sector may indeed be crowding the private sector out, with resultant thinner markets and greater price volatility. The massive public housing supply is excluded from our analysis because it is not guided by market mechanisms. We see that there is a strong public-private duality in the housing sector today:

- In number of units the public and the private housing stocks are roughly equal with 853 000 public units and 886 000 private ones.

Table 1.1

Housing in Hong Kong: A Summary of the Composition of Stock

Year	Total Housing stock				Public housing			Private Housing							
	No. of units ('000)	% Growth	% Public	% Private	No. of units ('000)	% Growth	% owner-occupied	No. of units ('000)	% Growth	% owner-occupied	A	B	C (in thousand units)	D	E
1983	1063	–	–	–	517	–	5.0%	546	2.9%	56.8%	212	236	53	29	16
1984	1114	4.8%	49.5%	50.5%	551	6.6%	6.5%	563	3.1%	58.3%	227	236	54	30	16
1985	1168	4.9%	49.3%	50.7%	576	4.5%	8.3%	592	5.2%	60.5%	247	242	56	31	17
1986	1231	5.4%	49.2%	50.8%	606	5.2%	11.0%	625	5.6%	61.6%	264	253	58	32	17
1987	1294	5.1%	49.2%	50.8%	636	5.0%	12.6%	658	5.2%	66.9%	275	271	61	34	18
1988	1344	3.9%	48.5%	51.5%	652	2.5%	13.2%	692	5.2%	69.9%	286	287	64	36	19
1989	1410	4.9%	48.5%	51.5%	684	4.9%	14.3%	726	4.9%	71.8%	292	308	68	38	20
1990	1504	6.7%	47.9%	52.1%	721	5.4%	16.4%	783	7.9%	72.6%	301	351	72	39	20
1991	1530	1.8%	48.9%	51.1%	749	3.9%	17.9%	781	-0.2%	73.8%	304	341	75	40	21
1992	1586	3.6%	49.2%	50.8%	781	4.3%	19.2%	805	3.0%	76.0%	312	354	77	40	21
1993	1637	3.2%	49.1%	50.9%	804	2.9%	20.7%	833	3.4%	74.2%	323	370	78	41	21
1994	1696	3.6%	48.9%	51.1%	830	3.2%	23.0%	866	4.0%	74.5%	332	389	82	43	21
1995	1739	2.5%	49.1%	50.9%	853	2.8%	22.9%	886	2.3%	74.4%	335	400	86	44	21

Notes: Private stock categories – Class A: smaller than 40 m²; Class B: 40–70 m²; Class C: 70–100 m²; Class D: 100–160 m²; and Class E: larger than 160 m².
Source: La Grange, A.R. (1996). Centre for Urban planning and Environmental Management, The University of Hong Kong; Rating and Valuation Department.

- In terms of gross floor area (GFA) the private stock is almost twice as large as the public one with approximately 45.5 million m² against 24.9 million m². The average private unit has about 55 m² and the public one only 29 m² of gross floor area.
- With the commencement of the privatization policy in 1976, the share of the public stock under privatization at subsidized prices (mostly through land prices below market) has grown to about 23% of the public units.
- About 51% of the total population owns or rents a privately supplied housing unit to which should be added around 11% acceding to ownership via public programs.
- The average rent to income ratio (RIR) (including rates, rent, management, water and power) diverges sharply between the public sector with 8.4% and the private sector where it is four times larger with 32.7% (see Chapter 3).

We are not claiming that such large-scale government intervention has not had the potential to distort the private market. The FDW model can help report the nature, direction and impact of these distortions but it is beyond the scope of this book to identify the nature and extent of such distortions. To establish the nature and extent of such possible distortions for Hong Kong would require fundamental and empirical research beyond the present scope of this study.

Organization of the Book

The preparation of this book was guided by three principal objectives. Firstly, it was to apply the Fisher-DiPasquale-Wheaton (1992) two-sector, four-quadrant model of a real estate economy in order to identify the *key factors* which shape the *dynamics* of the private residential real estate market in Hong Kong; secondly, to do brief experiments to test the model's ability to assess the potential impact of public policy towards the industry. In conducting the experiments we aim to test the internal consistency of the model, and as such do not expect readers to agree with our view of the adjustment mechanism as we perceive it — our main purpose is to test the organizing power of the framework, but if our analyses generate debate it would achieve an additional but unintended aim. As the third objective, we attempted to identify and describe relationships and institutions with a minimum of technical analysis, in order to provide accessibility to as wide an audience as possible, including professionals active in the real estate markets of Hong Kong, investment research analysts in the financial sector in Hong Kong and other world financial sectors, corporate executives in the real estate sector in Hong Kong and other economies, policymakers in Hong Kong and other jurisdictions, and also members of the general public with a personal or household interest in this important economic sector of Hong Kong.

In conducting our analyses, we have followed closely the organization of the FDW model itself, and present our findings in eight chapters. In Chapter 2, we present some stylized facts of Hong Kong and its residential real estate sector primarily to serve as background to readers that are not familiar with Hong Kong. Following that, Chapter 3 focuses on the real estate market and identifies key factors which shape the demand for residential real estate space in Hong Kong as well as the allocation and pricing of available space. Chapter 4 covers the links between the real estate economy and the Hong Kong financial markets, and valuation and investment decisions. Chapter 5 focuses on the production process and the physical, regulatory and economic factors that shape the structure and organization of the Hong Kong real estate industry and its output. Finally, closing this four-part decomposition of the real estate economy, Chapter 6 highlights the key features of the stock adjustment process in Hong Kong and the factors which explain the rapidly changing composition of its real estate stock over time. Chapter 7 suggests how the model can be used in the evaluation of public policy, and precedes a short conclusion (Chapter 8).

Throughout the analysis we have attempted to concentrate on the identification of critical relationships, institutions and structural phenomena that cause participants in the industry to behave in particular ways. In the end, our conclusion is that if the FDW model performs well in the organization of relationships in the residential sector, and the lessons learnt should prove invaluable to the analysis of all sectors of Hong Kong's real estate economy.

Note

1   Fund management and investment trust legislation in Hong Kong at present does not allow direct investment in real estate assets. It is our understanding that this is presently under review. However, trust legislation allows a limited proportion of investment in unlisted real estate securities, of which there exists a few current real estate lease — or mortgage-backed securities issues in Hong Kong.

Plate 4 Housing Delivery at Scale
The Hong Kong real estate industry is one of the most sophisticated in the world. New comprehensively planned developments on greenfield sites allow supply at extensive project scale with extremely efficient, technology-intensive construction methods and significant scale economies. It also results in a narrower range of delivery options and substantial barriers to entry. Greenfield sites are becoming scarcer, and development focus is shifting to urban redevelopment.

Plate 5 Revelopment Pressures
Rapid change in the economic structure of Hong Kong has resulted in substantial industrial land with significant redevelopment potential. Facilitating the redevelopment of this land is a major public policy challenge over the next decade.

2 THE HONG KONG ECONOMY AND REAL ESTATE SECTOR: AN OVERVIEW

It can be argued that Hong Kong, as a world city concentrating on finance, information and trade has only three remaining strategic advantages in the economic competition between world cities; namely its resourceful and highly ingenious people, its well-developed and free port and location on the southern coast of China, and possibly the most open economy in a world that is still in the process of breaking down barriers to globalization. As a post-industrial economy, these factors make the utilization of Hong Kong's limited land resources extremely important for its continued economic success. This chapter provides background to Hong Kong's recent economic development and aims to present basic insights into the importance of its land resources to its economy. Against the background of a pending change in sovereignty with Hong Kong's return to China in July 1997 when Hong Kong becomes a Special Administrative Region (SAR) of the People's Republic of China, under the principle of 'one country, two systems', we also aim to identify and provide brief analyses of key economic institutions and policies in Hong Kong that have been instrumental to the spectacular economic development of this dynamic city in the past. Given Hong Kong's absolute lack of natural resources, it could be argued that its highly flexible people are its greatest asset, and its market-friendly economic institutions could be viewed as its greatest achievement and contributed greatly to its success.

To a greater or lesser extent, the content of this chapter is elaborated upon in detail in various sections of the chapters that follow. The information and limited analyses provided in this chapter are intended for readers with no or little knowledge of Hong Kong, and informed readers may wish to proceed to Chapter 3. To limit the length of the chapter, we also resort in part to presenting facts in point form.

History: Centrality of Hong Kong's Interaction with China[1]

Hong Kong has developed from a fragile, low-income entrepôt to China with some agricultural activities and support services industries in the 1950s, through a period of rapid industrialization in the 1960s and early 1970s, into a modern, high value added post-industrial services economy in less than two generations. In 1995, it had the most advanced employment structure of all economies in the world, with more than 80% of its economically active citizens employed in services industries and large proportions in high value added financial, professional and international trading services. At the time of writing, Hong Kong was the tenth largest trading economy in the world, and its per capita GDP at around US$23 000 was of the highest in the world and second highest in Asia after Japan. Hong Kong suffers acutely from land shortages, has no natural resources apart from its excellent deep water free port (the world's biggest container port), and its 6.4 million highly educated and ingenious people. It has run trade surpluses and government budget surpluses almost uninterruptedly for the last fifteen years, technically it has no government funding requirement (and often awkwardly, therefore, no credit rating), and has been a capital exporter for much of the last ten years.

It is of course incorrect to suggest that Hong Kong's recent economic development was not influenced by its location on the coast of Southern China and China's decision to concentrate on Southern China with its first industrial reforms in its declared 'Special Economic Zones' (one of which, Shenzhen, borders on Hong Kong and is a city of around 3 million people). Hong Kong's development as an export-led, light manufacturing economy up to the mid-1970s is well-documented and possibly more impressive than the development of the other three original Asian Tiger economies, because it happened substantially without any trade barriers (see Chau, 1993). After China's open-door policy and the commencement of economic reform in China's southern provinces, in particular Guangdong province which borders Hong Kong, its economy has functionally integrated with that of Southern China. Strongly influenced by this integration, Hong Kong's GDP expanded at an average rate of around 7% per annum between 1980 through 1991. With deepening of the economy, the Hong Kong GDP growth rate has stabilized around 5.5% per year. Through massive relocation of manufacturing from Hong Kong mostly into Guangdong province (and to an important but lesser extent, Thailand and Vietnam), Hong Kong's manufacturers have been taking advantage of cheaper labour elsewhere in the face of continued rapid increases in the cost of industrial labour in Hong Kong. It is estimated that Hong Kong companies have created around 6 million employment opportunities in Southern China alone; while most high value added business services and executive functions are controlled from Hong Kong and most final exporting occurs through Hong Kong's sea and airport. Hong Kong's engine of new growth over the last decade has been high value added financial and business services; and Hong Kong has become an essential source of technology and skills transfer for China. Thus Hong Kong has effectively become the business and financial centre of the functional and metropolitan Pearl River Delta area and the whole of Southern China, apart from being at the geographic centre of the whole southeast Asian economic region.

Throughout its brief history as a separately administered entity from China, Hong Kong's interactions with China have always been the fundamental and defining dimension around which all other aspects of Hong Kong socio-economic development revolve whether they are local, regional, or international (see Map 1). Historical milestones relevant to Hong Kong's land economy from the last 150 years include:

- **1841–1860–1898** Britain acquires successively Hong Kong Island (72 km²), the Kowloon Peninsula (7 km²) and the New Territories (933 km²). The Kowloon Peninsula and Hong Kong Island were originally ceded to Britain in perpetuity, while the New Territories were leased to Britain for 99 years, ending in 1997. These original, very exiguous 1012 km² of land have been marginally expanded over the years through land reclamation.

- **1951** The UN embargo on China trade at the time of the Korean war follows soon after the foundation of the People's Republic of China in October 1949 when movement between Guangdong and Hong Kong started to dwindle. This international UN decision totally stops the entrepôt trade and further severs most economic and social links between Hong Kong and its south China hinterland. Hong Kong is suddenly forced into precarious economic self-sufficiency and is described at that time as a society living on 'borrowed time in a borrowed place'.

- **1979** China's open-door policy leads to the rapid re-emergence of economic links with China. Hong Kong starts its reintegration with its hinterland and by the mid-1980s, there is significant relocation of Hong Kong's industrial activities into the Pearl River Delta and Guangdong province (and subsequently also to Vietnam, Thailand and Malaysia) to benefit from particularly advantageous labour and land costs. In the services sector, Hong Kong draws considerable economic benefits from being the main window between China and the rest of the world.

- **1984** The Sino-British Joint Declaration initiates the process of returning of Hong Kong to China. Annex III of the Declaration contains eight clauses which cover the use of land during the transition to 1997, including land leases that straddle 1997.[2] The fundamental legal and economic principles for this reunification and the functioning of Hong Kong as a 'Special Administrative Region' (SAR) are defined in the Basic Law which has since been drafted as Hong Kong's new constitution.

- **1997** Hong Kong will start operating under the principle of 'one country, two systems'. After being a British colony for more than a hundred and fifty years, and after operating for around fifty years as a functionally autonomous and self-contained city state trading worldwide (hence the often made analogy with Venice during the Renaissance), Hong Kong is to be reintegrated with China in 1997. From the viewpoint of an urban region, Hong Kong Island is rapidly evolving into the Manhattan of the Southern China urban and regional system.

For the purpose of this book, the relevant historical period is therefore 1951–1997. The continuation of the financial, economic, legal and regulatory features which have made the Hong Kong economy and real estate industry a world leader is an obvious cause of concern given the very wide gap which exists between Hong Kong and China's practices presently. For the real estate sector specifically, public concern exists about the possible erosion of Hong Kong legal and regulatory environment after 1997 through public interventions into market institutions that are not well understood.[3]

Geography: Very High Density of Urban Development

It is frequently remarked that geography is destiny, and this applies to Hong Kong at a macro and micro level. Its establishment on the south coast of China may have been historically opportunistic, but geography has since acted both to Hong Kong's advantage and disadvantage. Located on the southern coast of China on the fringes of the Pearl River Delta, it has an unsurpassed strategic economic location with the best deep-sea harbour along the entire coast of China, with an excellent location for international trade within Asia as well as between Asia and the rest of the world. These macro-locational advantages are balanced by an extremely difficult topography with 80% of Hong Kong's land area mountainous and hard to develop using conventional technologies, thus leading to very dense utilization and management of the portion of land resources that is conventionally developable. Map 2 illustrates clearly the topographical constraints to land development in Hong Kong. Important land management related aspects include:

- Land is the scarce factor in Hong Kong with the territory totalling around 1050 km², fragmented into more than 200 islands with a very high population density in its developed urban areas. In fact, Hong Kong has passed the 6 million population mark in 1994, ahead of projections. Map 2 also illustrates the increasing population pressure on Hong Kong's limited land. At present around 60% of Hong Kong's population reside in around 80 km², which is developed extremely densely (this is commonly referred to as Hong Kong's 'urban areas').[4]
- Managing high density is thus the central feature of Hong Kong urban planning. The major change that has taken place from earlier decades is from uncoordinated piecemeal real estate development to systematic and better integrated planning. Large, mixed-use development projects are a common feature of the real estate industry.

- Due to the constraints on land resources, competition for land among industrial, commercial, residential, infrastructure, environmental and recreational uses, and between personal and freight movement is among the most severe in Asian cities.[5] The opportunity cost of land in any use is extremely high and land typically represents around 60–70% of total real estate asset values in Hong Kong. These extremely high land values seriously complicate economic depreciation concepts when applied to real estate assets in Hong Kong.

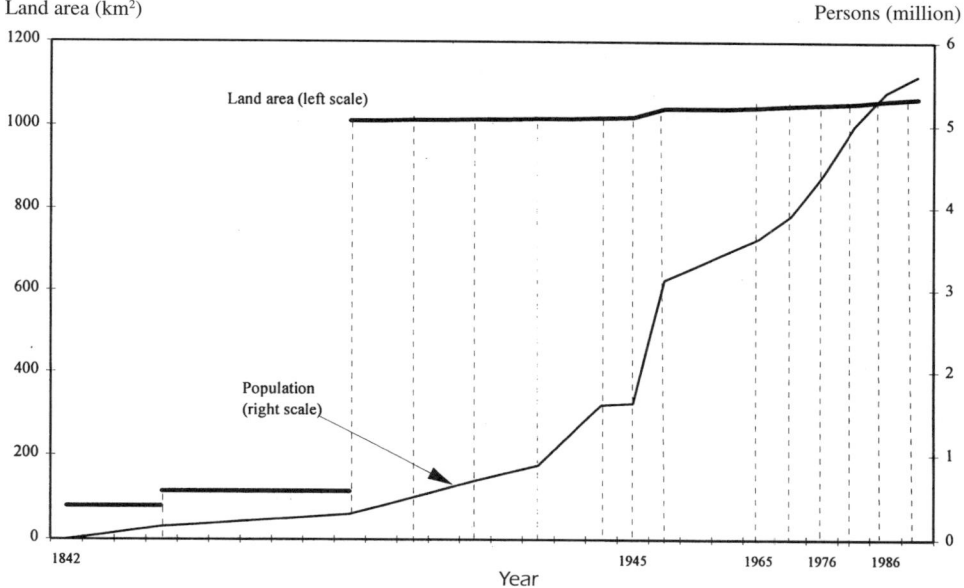

Source: Developed from Pryor and Pau in Lampugnagni (ed.), 1993: 111.

Figure 2.1   *Population and Land Area in Hong Kong since 1842*

- The management of land as a resource in Hong Kong deserves specific mention. Excluding negligible pockets of land, the Hong Kong government (until 1997, technically, the Crown) owns all land in the territory, and its management features prominently in public policy. Through its ownership of Crown land and the sale of land leases, the government plays a very active role in urban planning, infrastructure provision and social housing. New land leases are typically sold at public auctions.
- As a consequence, land is *the* strategic resource for real estate companies in Hong Kong. In spite of the high cost of land, the constitution of private land reserves is a common practice by large real estate development companies. The sustained high rate of appreciation of land since 1950 has made such private land inventories

viable. Access to land is then also possibly the most critical barrier to entry into the real estate development industry and is certainly a critical factor in the continued operation and profitability of real estate development companies in Hong Kong. Its scarcity as well as the need for a countervailing power with the government has been a factor encouraging concentration in the real estate sector. The demand for the services of Hong Kong's real estate industry has changed according to Hong Kong's level of development and associated structural changes within the economy.

- The government has used the sale of land leases, a key public asset, for the dual purpose of generating a major share of its revenues and implementing core urban planning regulations. Most of these land sales are through public auctions, a minority are through closed tenders and 'private treaties'. Changes in land uses not permitted in an original lease lead to a lease renegotiation with the Land Department and the collection of a land 'premium' which is a form of tax on the change in land value (also known as 'betterment tax' in many other jurisdictions).

Geography might have bestowed a great advantage on Hong Kong with its extremely advantageous macro-location and excellent deep-sea harbour on the one hand, and reduced this advantage somewhat with inhospitable topography that mitigates against simple technical and physical development solutions on the other; but it could be argued that Hong Kong's economic and social institutions have little further to do with geography, and are possibly its greatest achievement and reason for success. We now take a brief look at a select number of these institutions.

Economy: Stable Institutions, Openness, Flexibility and Rapid Growth

An Open, Free Market Economy and Stable Institutions

From an economic point of view, the main factors behind Hong Kong's success against difficult odds since 1950 can be summarized to include clear private and public property right, a very flexible and reliable contractual environment, and a stable public policy environment based on a free, market-oriented and regulatory environment. There has been a clear contrast between perceived large *external* political risks (with a 'capital P') in the form of a variety of external shocks over fifty years in Hong Kong (see Figure 2.2); and the stability of the *internal* institutional and economic environment, with very small ('little p') political risks to erode the quality of the local economic environment. Through the serendipity of strong Chinese entrepreneurial skills, dynamism, flexibility and education interacting with a stable legal and administrative system, Hong Kong has grown into an extremely resilient economy with the flexibility required to overcome external shocks rapidly, as illustrated in Figure 2.2.

Several additional institutions are important and deserve to be identified. These include:

- There are no tariff or non-tariff trade barriers. Hong Kong as a free port is possibly the most open economy in the world. There is a highly competitive business environment where domestic and foreign firms compete to a very high extent on a level playing field.

- There is a low and very predictable domestic taxation system, with public expenditures (excluding financially autonomous but publicly owned enterprises) representing only 17–18% of GDP.

- There is full currency convertibility and an entirely open, sound and very competitive financial system (see Commissioner of Banking, Annual Report 1994).

- A stable currency has been achieved through the introduction in 1983 of the Linked Exchange Rate System, which is a modern version of earlier currency boards;[6] because of this currency stability the Hong Kong dollar is increasingly used as a medium of business transactions and a popular currency for holding financial claims in China.[7]

- The extent, volume, timeliness and reliability of publicly available economic information is very high.

Real GDP Growth (%)

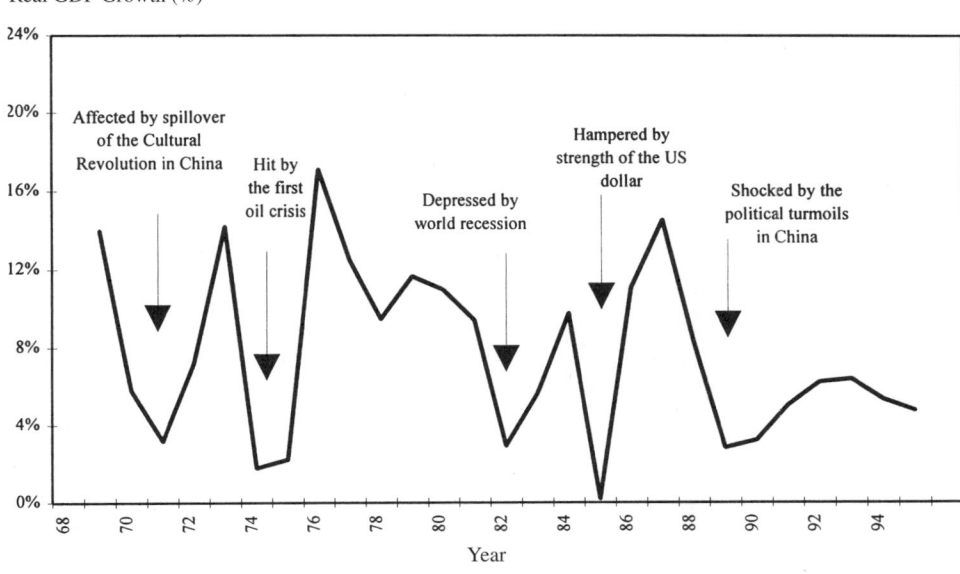

Source: Booz Allen and Hamilton analysis, government statistics.

Figure 2.2 A Resilient Hong Kong Economy, 1968–1995

There is a sound public-private sector balance. While the scope of government activities has increasing over time, especially after 1972, the policy environment remains dominated by a 'small government principle' and the government is committed to expanding its activities in line with GDP growth only. The *private provision of public services* is a well-established tradition. The government is attuned to private sector practices and public corporations are operated on a commercial basis including being listed on the Hong Kong Stock Exchange. Auctions and contestable markets for a wide variety of infrastructure and other public services are the rule.

High Growth Rates and a Rapidly Changing Economic Base

Hong Kong has transformed itself within only five decades from a fragile and developing low-income economy into a post-industrial society whose activities are increasingly intensive in human and physical capital. Continued growth depends on high value added activities, but against the backdrop of continued rapid structural changes. Selected structural developments and features of the Hong Kong's economy include:

- Light manufacturing for export was the mainstay of the Hong Kong economy from after the Second World War to around 1980. The number of registered factories exploded from 1266 registered factories in 1948 to 148 623 in 1986. Three quarters of factories employed fewer than nine people. Contracting and subcontracting dominated Hong Kong's industrialization. If we use a North American analogy, Hong Kong's industrialization was more easily comparable to that of Los Angeles than to that of Pittsburgh. There are very few industrial complexes and almost no factory chimneys in Hong Kong.
- With China's open-door policy and the resumption of sustained interactions with the mainland, Hong Kong's economic structure has changed dramatically. The economic reintegration with the hinterland, and the development of Shenzhen in particular, has reversed the growth of the manufacturing sector. Industrial employment has fallen by 50% from 900 000 workers in 1984 to 450 000 in 1993 (*The Other Hong Kong Report*, 1994). Fu (1995) estimates that while Hong Kong lost some 445 000 manufacturing employment opportunities during the years since 1987, some 580 000 employment opportunities were created in the banking and finance sector alone during the same period. (A glimpse into the dramatic structural changes over 1980–1994 is offered in Table 3.1). Hong Kong has also been playing a pivotal role in the rapid expansion of the various economic components of 'greater China'. Today, 70% of overseas investment in China is from Hong Kong, and 50% of China's foreign exchange enters through Hong Kong (*The Other Hong Kong Report*, 1993 and Walker et al., 1995). The Hong Kong economy is thus undergoing a major structural adjustment with its

reconnection to its hinterland. However, it continues to be export-led with a dramatic changes in the ratio of exports to re-exports (Figure 2.3).

HK$ billion in constant 1990 prices

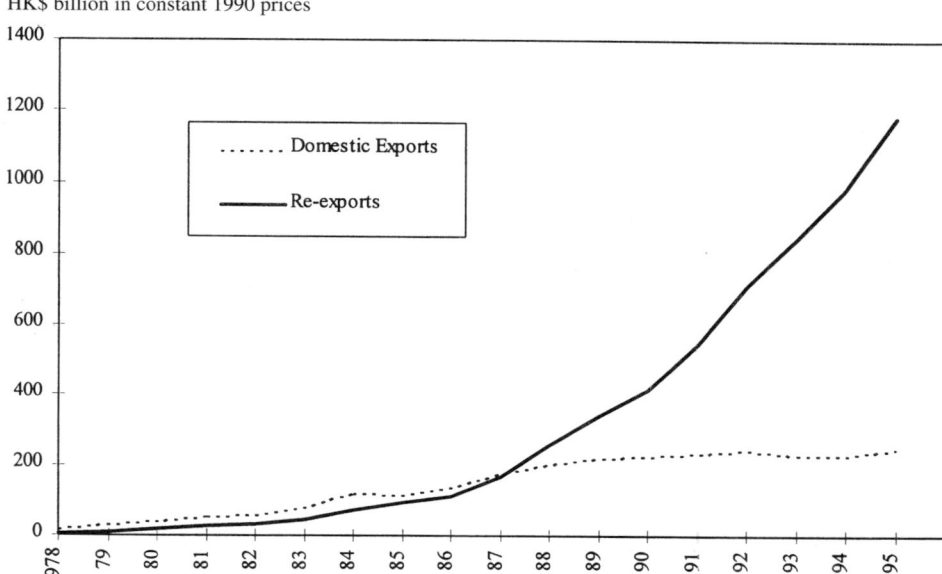

Source: Hong Kong Census and Statistics Department.

Figure 2.3　Hong Kong's Domestic Exports and Re-exports, 1982–1995

Table 3.1
Changes in the Hong Kong Employment Structure, 1980–1995

	1980	1985	1990	1995
	% share of total employment			
Manufacturing	**50.1**	**42.2**	**31.3**	**16.1**
Textile	7.0	5.5	4.4	2.5
Wearing apparel	14.4	13.2	9.2	3.4
Other manufacturing	28.7	23.5	17.8	10.2
Services	**44.3**	**53.9**	**65.1**	**80.4**
Wholesale and retail trades; restaurant and hotel	24.8	29.9	36.3	43.8
Transport, storage and communication	4.0	4.7	5.8	7.4
Financing, insurance, real estate and business services	6.5	9.0	12.1	16.3
Community, social and personal services	9.1	10.2	10.9	13.0

Source: Hong Kong Monthly Digest of Statistics.

- Investment efficiency has been high due to the effective public-private partnership, low-cost contracting and innovative production. National accounts show that total factor productivity in Hong Kong has been extremely high and that Hong Kong has achieved the same long-term rate of economic growth as Singapore (at around 7.5% per annum) over the period 1960–1990 but at a much lower cost. To sustain its high growth, Hong Kong has invested only 25% of its GDP when Singapore needed a 40% investment rate, i.e. one-third more (see Young, 1992). In recent years, with the deepening of the economy, the Hong Kong GDP growth rate has stabilized around 5.5% per year. However, with the growing earnings from the Pearl River Delta hinterland activities and other investments in Asia and worldwide, the GNP growth rates are most likely higher.

- Hong Kong is a prime example of an 'incubator economy' where firm size is small, and innovation and employment mobility rates are high. In spite of its compactness, the annual rate of relocation of employment which is not recorded must be very high for both services and manufacturing. In a typical developing city like Bogota, about 5–7% of the jobs relocate every year (Lee, 1989), whereas in mature urban economies the rate is usually around 2–3%. In Hong Kong, it can be expected that the internal job mobility rate will be higher than in developing cities.

- With the economic structure of Hong Kong changing to become a post-industrial services and international trade based economy against other world cities, the importance of its natural harbour as a critical strategic asset with its supporting infrastructure is fully recognized by the government and the community. It is also consequently recognized that Hong Kong's air and sea transport infrastructure plays and will continue to play a fundamental role in maintaining continued competitiveness in the world economy. Infrastructure spending is therefore essential to maintaining Hong Kong competitiveness as a trading economy. Annual investment in infrastructure has fluctuated around 4–5% of GDP with the development of a new airport and expansion of existing seaport facilities totalling about US$20 billion.[8] Whereas in developing countries, public infrastructure is generally around 90% provided by the public sector. A very high share of 40% is provided by the private sector in Hong Kong, and within the private share, much is provided under build-operate-transfer terms that imply an ultimate reversion to public ownership. Ineffective coordination for air and sea transport investments made by Chinese authorities within the Pearl River Delta has been a serious concern over much of the last decade. There have been, however, recent improvements in the coordination of infrastructure development in the Pearl River Delta (reported in *International Business Week*, 20 January 1997).

It can be expected that the influence of this changing economic base on the real estate industry is very large. Existing structures have rapidly become economically obsolete or must adjust to changes in uses. Local areas face large shifts in personnel and freight movement. The need for costly urban redevelopment as opposed to greenfield development brought about by economically obsolete structures is accordingly large. Looking at the industrial sector alone, there is rapid obsolescence of traditional buildings, with new distribution functions forcing changes from bulk warehousing to more sophisticated, specialized facilities. This pattern of a changing structure of demand affects all sectors, as the demand for real estate services increasingly shifts to the production of high value added goods and services, the so-called 'quaternary sector' and the demands of people employed in this sector.

The Hong Kong Real Estate Industry

The rapidly changing Hong Kong economy the development of the functional Southern China economy have resulted in a significant role for the real estate and construction sectors of Hong Kong. Also, the rapid changes outlined above demanded exceptional performance from the industry as Hong Kong's stock of real estate assets and infrastructure is restructured — and the industry has delivered following these demands. For example, in 1995 it was estimated that the real estate and construction sectors in Hong Kong's economy contributed on average over 24% to GDP since 1980. It was further estimated that in the private sector a liberal analysis of consolidated and unconsolidated corporate shareholding on the Hong Kong Stock Exchange suggested that the real estate and construction sectors represented some 45% of stock market capitalization, while in the public sector approximately 33% of government revenue comes from real estate and construction (Walker et al., 1995).

In sum, the importance of real estate and developments affecting the real estate market and real estate values cannot be exaggerated. Sustaining the performance of the real estate industry is, therefore, a major public policy concern. Following Walker et al. (1995), a few key indicators of the relative size and importance of the sector in the economy are:

- During 1983–92 an average of 61% of capital investment was in real estate.
- Although the real estate share of GDP is cyclical, it has averaged over 24% since 1980.
- The real estate and construction share of total stock market capitalization is conservatively estimated at 45%. In the US this share is under 5% and in the UK it is under 10%. In emerging Asian markets it ranges between about 10% and 20%.
- Market capitalization trends on the Hong Kong Stock Exchange show that real

estate is second only to 'consolidated enterprises' which themselves include a significant real estate component. This capitalization share is larger than that of financial shares.

- Over 35% of bank lending is to the real estate and construction sector (which in itself is a cause for concern elaborated upon in later chapters).
- Over 33% of government revenues comes from real estate and construction related items. Almost 35% of government expenditure is on real estate, mostly infrastructure and housing.

The deepening of the real estate economy in Hong Kong is suggested by the fact that by 1993 the real estate stock per capita was estimated to be HK$550 000 per person (US$71 000) and about HK$1 100 000 per economically active person (US$142 000). These magnitudes exclude the wide variety of government buildings as well as civil engineering infrastructure.

Analyses of the Hong Kong industry usually differentiate five real estate market sectors:[9]

- offices
- retail
- industrial and warehousing
- residential
- hotels

Barriers to entry into all sectors are high and rising. Among these barriers are the extremely high level of capital required to bid for land, the prevalence of capital-intensive high-rise technologies, and the need to finance large and mixed-use projects. As a result the real estate development industry has become highly concentrated, but there are also increasing pressures towards further concentration in the industry (the industry and its structure is analysed in more depth in Chapter 5).

It is an important feature of the Hong Kong real estate industry that a significant amount of business concentration among developers co-exists with an extremely decentralized construction industry. The average size of firms remains very small at under 8 workers per firm, together with a substantial number of large and extremely competitive and sophisticated principal contractors. This apparent contradiction derives from the extremely high quality and efficiency of contracting and construction project management in Hong Kong, which permits large projects to be finely subcontracted and be extremely cost-competitively executed.

A business factor common to all five sectors caused by structural changes in the economy briefly described above, is that Hong Kong has moved into an era of high cost urban redevelopment, which makes high quality supply a necessity. Urban development has shifted from *greenfield development* to *urban restructuring* and the public sector is taking an active role in leading this redevelopment through public/ private sector redevelopment vehicles such as the Land development Corporation. In residential areas three typical problems are the shortage of land which produced excessively high densities, parcel fragmentation inherited from uncoordinated earlier development, and the inadequate provision of open space and amenities demanded by a high-income population. Major public policy challenges for 2000 to 2015 include severe constraints faced in the redevelopment of old industrial areas (for example Kwai Chung and Kwun Tong) and other sites that were previously used for oil storage, dockyards, power stations, railway yards, military bases, and soon an airport and its ancillary facilities.

Frictions in the urban restructuring process have led to the creation of a joint public-private vehicle, the Urban Land development Corporation whose main object is to lower the cost and shorten the time required for land consolidation through the use of public powers linked to the leasehold system — 'land resumption' in Hong Kong terminology (see Chapter 6).

Concluding Remarks

As has been mentioned, the purpose of this chapter is to provide brief historical and relevant background information to interpret analyses that follow in subsequent chapters. In the process we have outlined, in truncated fashion, the dramatic changes that have occurred in the Hong Kong economy over the last five decades. It has been fortunate that the social cost of this transition was limited with low unemployment during the rapid change. The Hong Kong economy actually experienced an overall labour shortage while it underwent the rapid structural change from a light manufacturing economy to an economy based on the delivery of high-order services in international trade and finance.

The spectacular performance of the Hong Kong economy over the last three decades has been evident of its two most important resources: its people and its economic and social institutions. The extraordinary flexibility and adaptability exhibited by the transformation of the economy over some fifteen years from being dominated by manufacturing employment to being overwhelmingly dominated by high-order services is possibly the most telling example to date in world economic history of just how flexible human resources are when allowed to respond to economic challenges without restriction. We then also have to point out that people cannot achieve such extraordinary flexibility and creativity without institutions that encourage and support flexibility and mobility — good education, open and freely contestable markets, labour mobility, rapid and free-flowing information of a high quality. These institutions are possibly Hong Kong's greatest achievement, and the extent to which they are preserved (and improved, or otherwise) after 1997 remains a question. An important further question concerns the extent to which Hong Kong has succeeded in building up a lasting comparative advantage in advanced services over other major Asian cities in finance, trade and transportation, telecommunications, real estate services, other business services, and high value added goods (see Krugman, 1993).

To conclude, this chapter provided important insights into some of characteristics and institutions that contributed greatly to Hong Kong's economic success. Facts, insights and speculations presented in this chapter will be returned to and elaborated upon where necessary within discussions of the various aspects of the FDW model in the following chapters.

Notes

1   This is drawn in part from Hakfoort and Pretorius, 1996.
2   For overviews of the land system, see Leung (1986) and Walker and Flanagan (1990). Two important aspects of Annex III for the behaviour of the real estate economy are the agreement to cap annual sales of leases to 50 hectares per year, and the scale of the premium to be charged on the change of use in existing leases (par. 5). The cap on the sale of land leases was found to be too restrictive and has been applied flexibly. On the other hand, there is a real concern that the premium on change of use is a poorly framed 100% redevelopment tax with increasingly negative impacts on urban redevelopment and the supply of new buildings. Its effect is to restrict redevelopment to existing leases conforming to intended new uses. A confiscatory level of the redevelopment premium can only shrink the value of land inventories in an environment of already scarce supply (*South China Morning Post*, 21 September 1994).
3   Misguided interventions by officials whether elected or appointed are a permanent threat to well-functioning real estate markets everywhere, because real estate assets are the longest lived investments in the economy possibly with the exception of physical infrastructure. To strengthen their own political position, officials who have a limited tenure may make short-term decisions that can negatively affect the sector for decades. Such decisions may be very difficult to reverse as their beneficiaries become politicized and vocal. Economists describe this gap between the public good and private interests as a 'principal-agent' or 'agency' problem. This problem is particularly acute in the housing sector because of its political sensitivity.
4   We follow Hau (1992) in defining Hong Kong's urban areas as the built-up areas of Hong Kong Island, Kowloon, Tsuen Wan and Kwai Chung. This represents about 80 km² and around 60% of the population reside in these areas (see Map 2). However, it must be pointed out that the proportion of total population presently residing in the New Territories has grown from around 20% in 1971 to around 40% at present with the development of new towns in the New Territories, while the absolute number of residents living in the urban areas has remained approximately static at around 3.5 million.
5   The urban planning experience of Hong Kong is very valuable for major Chinese cities. These cities experience extremely high population densities not only because of increasing rural-urban migration but also because of severe underinvestment in municipal infrastructure between 1940 and 1980. Practically no investment in either infrastructure or housing took place during the ten years of the Cultural Revolution (1966–76) and very little until the early 1980s (see Bertaud, 1994).
6   See Hong Kong Monetary Authority, 1993.

7   By the third quarter of 1993, Hong Kong bank claims on China represented slightly more than 10% of the Hong Kong broad money supply. Some 90% of these claims are held by 24 banks. (See Yam, in HKMA, 1994a.)

8   The new Chek Lap Kok Airport on Lantau Island is the largest single infrastructure project in the world at the time of writing. Yet its cost represents less than a third of the total infrastructure investment planned for Hong Kong. Hong Kong is already the largest container port in the world, while the present Kai Tak Airport reached total saturation in 1995 for passenger and freight traffic. At one time it was handling up to 20% of the entire world air cargo traffic in a single day.

9   For basic information on each of these five sectors see Walker and Flanagan, 1991. Periodical updates on each of these five sectors are produced by Hong Kong real estate consulting firms. See, for instance the Hong Kong section of *Asia Pacific Trends, Conditions and Forecasts* by Colliers-Jardine Research, July 1994, Edition 6; and various editions of the *Jones Lang Wootton Pacific Digest* and the *JLW Property Indices for Hong Kong*.

Plate 6 New ...
Rapid increases in household wealth have brought about rapid changes in taste and preferences for amenity. Current preferences in demand for housing, for owner-occupation or rental, is for comprehensively planned housing developments with integrated facilities. Development scale allows a variety of facilities and amenities to be integrated economically into the developments. This illustrates South Horizons, a popular location on Ap Lei Chau, off Hong Kong Island at Aberdeen.

Plate 7 ... AND OLD
Although it is part of the housing stock, older housing such as these in Kennedy Town on Hong Kong Island cannot compete with new tastes. Land assembly for redevelopment of older stock is extremely difficult under circumstances of fragmented ownership of housing within older buildings and older neighbourhoods.

3 THE PRICING AND ALLOCATION OF SPACE IN HONG KONG (QUADRANT 1)

In this chapter, a number of salient features of the behaviour of the private residential market in Hong Kong are discussed. These include the presentation of an introductory analysis of the rental market performance when compared to behaviour predicted by theory, prior to presenting an analysis of how the rental market performance contributes to the determination of asset prices (Chapter 4). In particular, four questions are addressed:
- What determines rents, i.e. the pricing of residential space?
- How responsive are rents to changing market conditions?
- Why is the rent level high in Hong Kong?
- Is there any evidence of a worsening rent situation?

The analysis below shows that the adjustment process in the rental market for housing services has been extremely efficient over the period from 1980 to 1995. It is also shown that despite high rates of growth in rentals, income growth over the same period has been correspondingly high, thus resulting in relative stability in aggregate measures of housing affordability as measured by rent-to-income ratios. Furthermore, questions about the divergence between residential rental growth and growth in asset prices are also raised and elaborated upon in Chapter 4, where we introduce complications in the housing asset price formation process brought about by households' tenure choice to owner-occupy rather than rent.

In this chapter, we concentrate on factors that affect demand for rental accommodation, and how the residential rental market has behaved over the 1985–1995 period. The overall impression is that private residential rental levels in Hong Kong adjust extremely rapidly to changes in market conditions. It has been proposed that such rapid adjustments are a hallmark of the allocational and price efficiency of the market.[1] We view the efficiency of the rental market as a consequence of the economic institutions in Hong Kong that do not function to frustrate tenant mobility, but also introduce a note of caution about the shrinking relative proportion of the rental sector in favour of the possibly less flexible tenure option of home ownership. Although this chapter presents an analysis of the residential rental market, the rental market for commercial and industrial property adjusts equally rapidly and efficiently, and also exhibits similar high tenant mobility.

The Determination of Rents in the FDW Model

The determination of the rental income that a real estate asset generates is simply the process of price formation for the flow of services that it generates. Housing services include shelter, recreation, locational advantages and preferences, family activities, and so on; and if they were quantified over the economic life of the housing unit, it should equate to the present price of the asset (Pozdena, 1988). Price formation is discussed in Chapter 4.

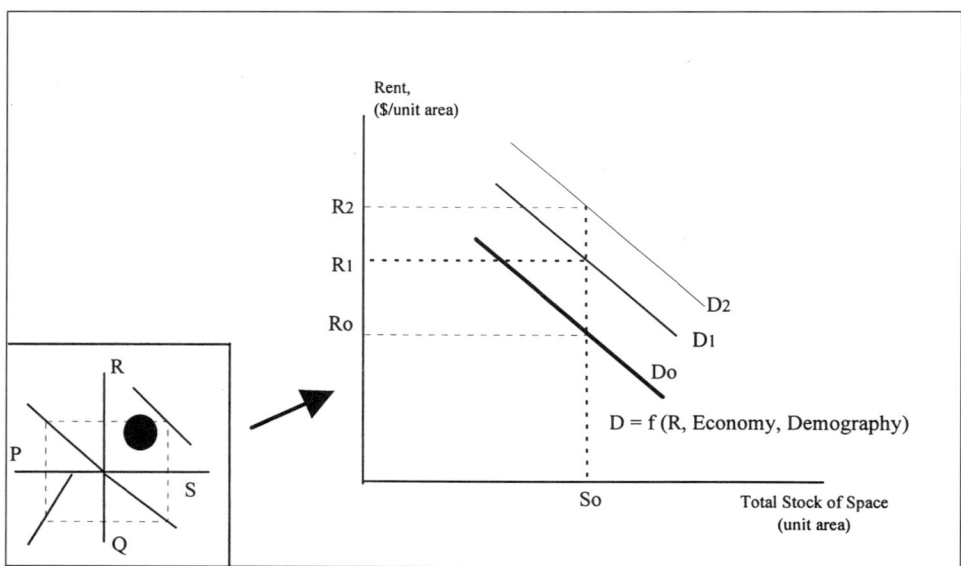

Figure 3.1 Quadrant 1 — The Determination of Rents

Figure 3.1 represents the determination of rents in the market for the services provided by real estate assets. Curve D_o illustrates a typical demand curve for the use of space offered by real estate assets. The overall level of demand for the services flowing from real estate space as an input into economic processes, relative to the supply of this space, would determine the level of rent R per unit area commanded by the space. With an ability to pay higher rents, perhaps through increased household earnings, the curve D_0 would tend to shift upwards (D_1) and with a fixed supply during that period this will result in higher rent (R_1). If there was an aggregate increase in demand, the demand curve would shift to the right (D_2) and rent levels will rise (R_2) should supply remain static.

Given the relatively fixed supply of housing in the short-term, the model suggests the following causal ordering of rent formation:

- *Shifts in demand* which in Hong Kong originate from two main groups of users: demographic trends including migration and household formation in Hong Kong; and to a lesser extent from movements in both international corporate staff and mainland Chinese state corporations staff.
- These shifts in demand on the existing stock of housing result in changes in *the vacancy rate*.
- The *rent level* adjusts in response to the changing vacancy rate.

We broadly follow this process in the analysis discussed below. However, in addition to the influence of public housing in the private sector housing market already mentioned, further phenomena exist in the private rental market that should be identified at this early stage. These are:

- Regulatory distortions of the private housing sector through rent control which came to Hong Kong from the UK in 1921 under the Landlord and Tenant Ordinance have de facto disappeared together with the housing stock of pre-World War II vintage. However, the tenancy protection parts of this act still have some effects on the behaviour of the private rental market and, therefore, at the margin on vacancy rates. There is no rent or security of tenure regulation in the non-residential sectors.
- An important and negative structural change in the Hong Kong housing market is the rapid disappearance of the private rental sector. Private rental tenure has declined from 30% in 1970 to less than 10% today. The implications of such a trend are important and should be analysed for Hong Kong, because international experience indicates that with the decline of the private rental sector, labour mobility by young, low- and middle-income households become impaired. In terms of the aggregate number of households in Hong Kong, the number in private residential tenancy is therefore quite small, albeit a very active proportion of the housing sector. The public rental sector is not a substitute for private rental markets because it has a very low mobility rate and long waiting lists.

Dynamics of Housing Demand

Shifts upward and to the right in the demand for private housing space by local Hong Kong residents have been very powerful. During the two decades 1975–95, the population has grown by 30% while real per capita GDP has tripled (see Figure 3.2). Population growth was 1.3% per annum during the period 1980–95 and includes substantial net immigration particularly since 1990. The population expanded from 5.04 million in 1980 to over 6 million in 1995.

Aggregate population expansion and growth in income, however, do not give an adequate indication of the importance of household formation on the demand for housing services. Over the same period the rate of household formation has been far more rapid at 4.9% per annum than total population growth, primarily due to the large proportion of the population in the age group of natural household formation (i.e. between 25–44 years old) and the shrinking of household size (see Figure 3.2) coupled with high rates of growth in household income. Population growth and the rate of household formation are compared in Figure 3.3. The supply of private housing grew slightly slower than household formation at 4.8% during the same period and that the public housing stock itself grew at 4.9% (see Table 1.1). During the period 1990–1994, there was an additional increase in the demand for housing services from returning migrants.

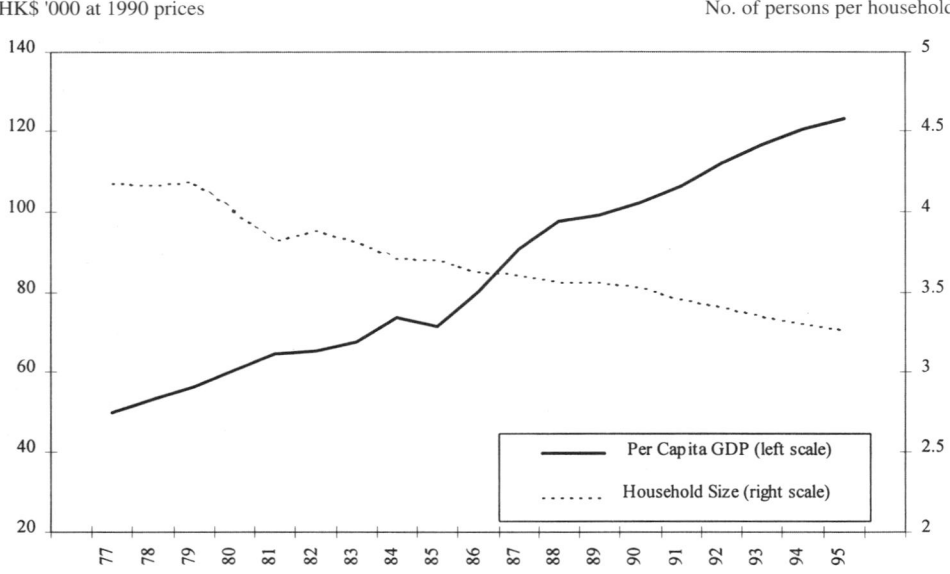

Source of data: Census and Statistics Department.

Figure 3.2　Per Capita GDP Growth and Change in Household Size

Source of data: Census and Statistics Department.

Figure 3.3 Growth in Population and Rate of Household Formation

    The above statistics suggest a rapidly increasing demand for housing services from a society with rapidly changing household structure and robustly growing household income. The income elasticity of demand for housing services has also therefore been predictably high in Hong Kong. There are only a few estimations of the demand for housing units by Hong Kong residents, of which attempts at comparative analyses of Hong Kong, Taiwan and Singapore by Tse (1994) is notable. His results suggest that the income elasticity of housing demand in Hong Kong is both high and larger than in either Taiwan or Singapore. He finds that the demand price-elasticity is unitary and the adjustment of demand to rising incomes is rapid in Hong Kong, and the fastest among the three economies. The most carefully specified model of the private Hong Kong housing market so far is by Peng (1993), and Peng and Wheaton (1994). Their aggregate demand estimates for the entire private sector concur with Tse's findings. They estimate that the income elasticity of demand for housing services in Hong Kong has a very high value of 2.39 which is much higher than in Japan, the US or Canada. They find that the demand elasticity is essentially unitary at –0.97. This price sensitivity would place Hong Kong in the higher range of international country values (Peng and Wheaton, 1994, Table 4).

    In conclusion, research confirms what theory predicts: in Hong Kong, rapidly rising incomes and high rates of household formation has created a high demand for increased services to flow from housing. An efficient and rapidly adjusting rental market has delivered this demand, and this is elaborated below.

Rent Flexibility and Hong Kong's Natural Vacancy Rate

To determine how private rentals have behaved in Hong Kong over the last fifteen years in response to changes in demand, one can use the familiar concept of 'natural vacancy rate' (Rosen and Smith, 1983). The concept of vacancy rate is central to the analysis of the dynamics of rents in every sector of the real estate market. It reflects two central adjustment mechanisms in a sector defined by immovable real estate. Firstly, it is easy to change the amount of vacant space at a given period of time but very difficult to change the total amount of space because supply takes time to respond to changes in market conditions; and secondly, buildings may not be movable, but through the functional relationship between rents and vacancy rates, vacancy rates become the critical mechanism through which space is also reallocated throughout the Hong Kong territory — and now beyond the border into the Pearl River Delta (witness different vacancy rates in different locations as discussed in Chapter 6 — see Figure 6.3).

The 'natural vacancy rate' is to real estate what the concept of 'optimum inventory' is to a manufacturer. It is the economically most efficient way that the owner of a real estate portfolio can serve his clientele in the most timely and efficient fashion under stable conditions. Far from being an indicator of waste, it reflects the most efficient aggregate inventory level to serve the market. The critical role of vacancies can be illustrated by considering the quandary of public housing authorities, where a non-zero vacancy is considered politically unacceptable and a 'waste of resources' because waiting lists are caused by high rates of housing subsidies. When the vacancy rate is zero nobody can move, and it is almost impossible for any family to adjust its consumption of services to its changing economic and/or demographic conditions. The natural vacancy rate is thus an aggregate indicator which reflects the constant turnover of units on the market.[2]

The natural vacancy rate theory holds that rents will adjust to changing market conditions according to the deviation of the observed vacancy rate from the underlying natural vacancy rate that is estimable but not directly observable. The rate of change of rents is expected to be proportional to the gap between the natural and the observed vacancy rate during the previous pricing period. It can be described simply by the following equation:

$$dR/R = \alpha \left(V_n - V_{t-1} \right) \tag{1.1}$$

dR/R represents the change in rents (**R**), α represents a constant estimated from market data, and **V** represents the vacancy rate in different periods. In principle, the higher the constant α, the larger will be the change in rent with deviations from the natural vacancy rate.

Tse (1994) tested various formulations of this basic rent adjustment model for Hong Kong. Hong Kong authorities monitor five categories of housing units according to size. (As stated in Chapter 1, housing units are aggregated into 'large apartments' (categories D and E) and 'small and medium' private apartments (categories A, B, and C).) The basic model presented above gives excellent statistical results in Hong Kong for the period 1980–1992. The estimated overall market vacancy rate is 4.2% (rounded from Tse's 4.17%, equation 1.26). Thus Hong Kong's aggregate vacancy rate is relatively low compared to housing results in the United States. Tse also estimates separate natural vacancy rates for the small-medium market ($V_n = 4.02$) and the large unit market ($V_n = 6.38$). As theory suggests, larger units have larger vacancy rates.[3]

Rents in Hong Kong are very responsive to changing market conditions and deviation of observed vacancy rates from the underlying 'natural' vacancy rate, and the aggregate vacancy rate model gives a good account of the year-to-year rates of rent changes. The adjustment factor ($\alpha = 7.2$ indicates that rents will rise by a factor of seven when the gap between the *observed* vacancy rate and the *underlying* natural vacancy rate deteriorates by one percent.[4] Figure 3.4 matches the actual year to year increases in aggregate market rent (rent in year 't') with the deviation of the actual vacancy rate from the underlying natural rate the preceding year (vacancy rate in year 't–1'). The evidence shows that the Hong Kong housing rental market clears very quickly and that rents are very flexible. It is also argued that like other segments of the Hong Kong real estate market, private housing is also subject to an important level of short-term 'volatility'. Such rent volatility could be attributed to two factors: first, the overall GDP volatility (Figure 2.3 in Chapter 2); and second, the crowding-out of private housing by the public housing sector and the undermining of the private rental market (see tenure trends in Figure 3.5). However, we also note again that an important consideration in interpreting this 'volatility' is actually the rapid rate at which the rental market adjusts. Fluctuations in housing assets price are discussed in Chapter 4.

Rental contracts are regulated in Hong Kong but there is no rent control.[5] Housing rents are both highly flexible upwards and downwards as is observable during 1982–84 when nominal rents actually declined substantially. This can possibly be explained by the custom of mostly short lease contracts for all forms of land use in Hong Kong (residential leases very seldom exceed two years). This has the consequence of a comparatively increased number of rental transactions over economies with longer customary lease contract periods, and consequently a shorter lag in rental price adjustment based on demand/supply mismatches in the market. We should point out

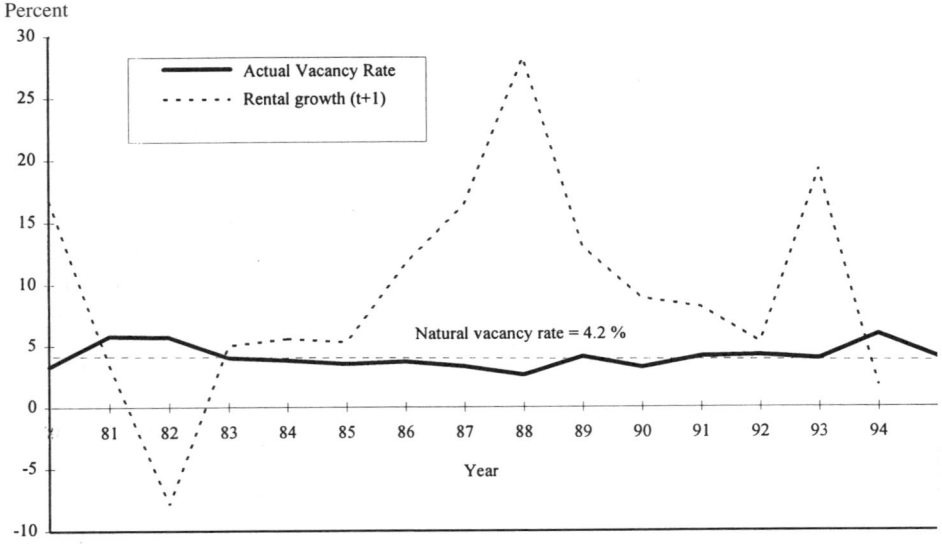

Sources: Rating and Valuation Department; Tse (1994).

Figure 3.4 Observed Vacancy Rate, Natural Vacancy Rate and Rent Response

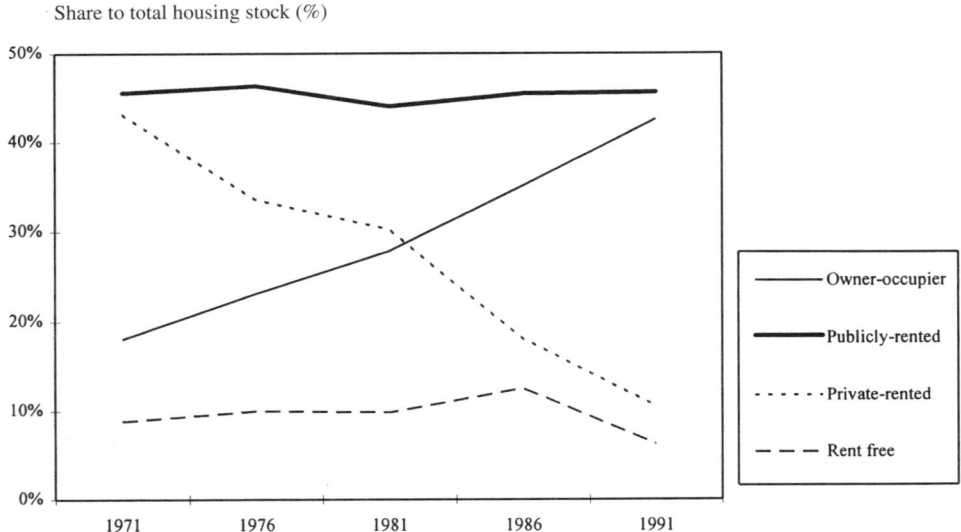

Source: Hong Kong Population Census 1991 Summary Report.

Figure 3.5 Dynamics of Housing Tenure in Hong Kong, 1971–1991

that price efficiency in the rental market is also improved by short contracts as a consequence of the rapid 'mark to market' effect that this creates with new transactions, as opposed to some countries where rental prices are sometimes distorted by price adjustments based on reported inflation over longer contracts or 'upward-only' rent review conditions in longer contracts. Another important consideration contributing to efficiency in the residential rental market is the relative homogeneity of the rental stock, thus creating a high degree of substitutability which contributes to tenant mobility.

Why is the Rent Level High in Hong Kong?

An important reason for international interest in Hong Kong is that it is one important model of urban development at high density, a common constraint in urbanizing Asia, particularly in China. High absolute rental price levels are consistent with the high opportunity cost of land and the high population densities in Hong Kong. For these reasons, the consumption of residential floor space per person remains low in Hong Kong in spite of the high per capita incomes. The high opportunity cost of land in residential use therefore demands that private housing must compete with other land uses for limited land; and for example when compared to retail land use it is difficult for housing rents to outbid dollar sales per square foot in central locations. As a consequence, private housing in Hong Kong is extremely expensive, with private 1996 rentals fluctuating around HK$20 000–30 000 (US$3000–4000) per month for residential units of approximately 70 m^2 in area in urban areas. The same properties traded at around HK$3–4 million, with well-located properties in sought-after developments selling for HK$5–6 million and more at that time. In early 1997, the range in monthly rentals per square foot was around HK$25–40 (US$3.20–5.15) on Hong Kong Island, HK$17–28 (US$2.18–3.6) in Kowloon, and HK$8–31 (US$1.03–4.00) in the New Territories. Figure 3.6 illustrates movements in Hong Kong residential rental and capital price indices for different categories from 1980 to 1995.

In addition to physical constraints, large-scale public housing provision is an extremely important distortion in the Hong Kong housing market. It is well-established that the effect of a large housing supply below market rent through direct public provision is to distort upwards the level of rent in the free sector (Fallis and Smith, 1984). It is possible to argue that one effect of the large supply of public housing has been to raise overall housing asset prices above the economically efficient price level indirectly. However, this point has yet to be investigated empirically for Hong Kong. The 50% share of public housing also raises important questions of intertemporal efficiency and equity that have yet to be considered seriously in Hong Kong (Hubert, 1993).

Index (1979 4th qtr = 100)

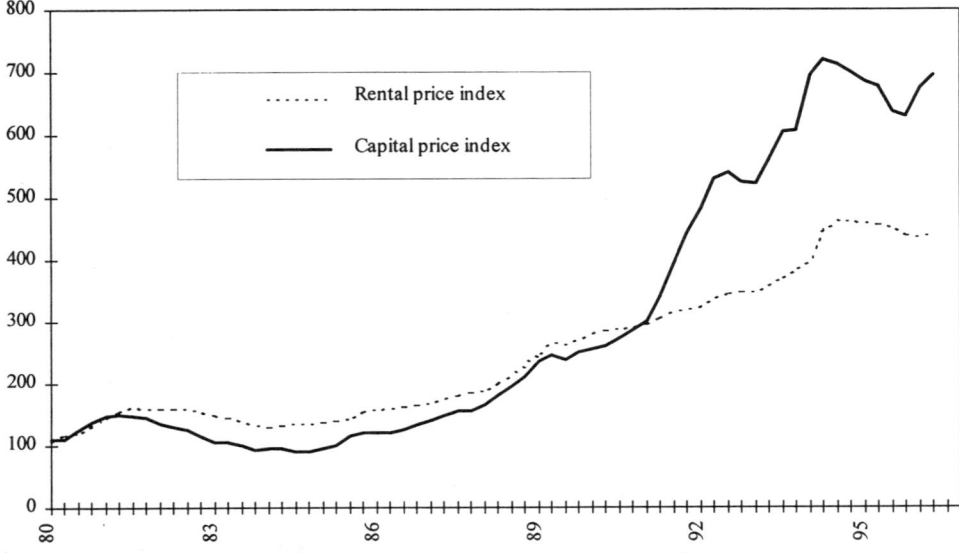

Source: Rating and Valuation Department.

Figure 3.6 Rental and Capital Price Indices, 1980–1995

Have Private Rental Conditions Deteriorated?

As Figure 3.6 shows, the residential price index for rents has increased by more than 400% between 1980 and 1995. From an international point of view, such rent price increases could lead to a deterioration of Hong Kong competitive position as location for international financial institutions and other types of service-oriented companies. However, it is not possible to derive strong conclusions from this rent price index for two reasons. First, it is not disaggregated and adjusted for quality changes, an important matter that will be examined in Chapter 6. Second, this is a nominal index and Hong Kong has experienced significant inflation that has risen close to 10% since the late 1980s, while real growth in residential rental prices have been approximately in line with real GDP growth in the economy. It therefore cannot be conclusively argued that rents have grown beyond households' capacity to pay. It is also difficult to tell whether the real price of quality adjusted services has risen significantly, nor by how much. What Figure 3.6 shows clearly, however, is that rates of increase in housing rents and housing asset prices have diverged sharply after 1990. This is a question to which we return in Chapter 4 where we analyse the process of residential asset price formation.

During the entire period 1980–1995, the demand for housing services by Hong Kong residents has shifted rapidly upwards and to the right with the growing population and rapidly rising real incomes. Notwithstanding the high absolute level of rentals, Figure 3.7 shows that the expenditure level for private housing services in the dominant small-medium housing market segment has remained broadly stable during the last decade in spite of the strong cycle experienced by the housing sector. The aggregate *rent-to-income ratio* (RIR) does not indicate a deterioration in the affordability of private housing services and by implication housing services consumption.

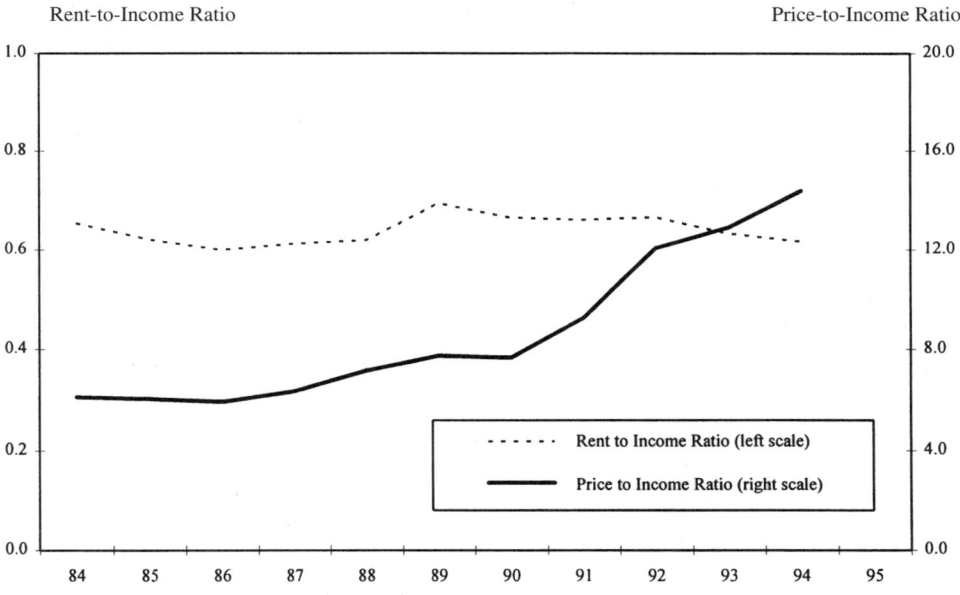

Source: R.L.H. Chiu, CUPEM, The University of Hong Kong.

Figure 3.7 *Housing Rent- and Price-to-Income Ratios, 1984–1994*

Concluding Remarks

In this chapter we showed that income growth and demographic factors in Hong Kong have been exerting an upward pressure on demand for housing space. More relevant to this study and the test of the FDW model, it has been shown as well that rental prices in Hong Kong are very responsive and have exhibited very rapid adjustment to changing market conditions. The efficiency and rapid price adjustment is an important characteristic of the residential rental market in Hong Kong, and despite the relatively small size of the market it behaves close to theoretical prediction. However, there are concerns at present over the shrinking of the proportion of housing stock available for private rental relative to the aggregate private housing stock, as similar conditions have created serious household mobility problems in other economies. It is uncertain whether these problems, for example most acutely experienced in the United Kingdom over the period 1990–1995, will be similar in a single metropolitan economy such as Hong Kong where geographical mobility is not so restrictive to economy. However, it has the potential to limit households' location preferences severely as the housing market matures and high transaction costs associated with changes in home ownership make moving less attractive. Therefore the relative reduction in the proportion of total stock in Hong Kong deserves to be viewed by policymakers with some concern, despite pressures that suggest home ownership remains the preferred tenure option in Hong Kong.

In the FDW model, the process of price determination for real estate services in the rental market directly affects the dynamics of real estate asset price formation. We now turn to this process.

Notes

1   This principle also applies to the market for housing assets in Hong Kong. The principle that high price variability and associated high transactions volume could also be a sign of an efficient market has frequently been pointed out by Anthony Darwell, a prominent real estate research analyst in Hong Kong.

2   As demonstrated by all socialist economies, even very low housing vacancy rates are a major cause of labour immobility, underemployment and/or unemployment (Mayo and Stein on Poland, 1988). In the case of Britain, the absence of a private rental market and long queues for council housing were estimated to have raised the unemployment rate by 1.2 percentage point in the 1980s (G. Hughes, 1989).

3   Observed and natural housing vacancy rates in housing tend to be smaller than in the office market. A primary reason is that both demand and housing units tend to be more standardized. In the US, observed office vacancies rates have varied greatly with business cycles. Hong Kong's housing supply consists of very homogenous apartment units concentrated in a small geographic area. The US supply consists of heterogeneous detached units across a continent.

4   In keeping with the debate on the theory underlying the natural vacancy rate paradigm, we do not propose that natural vacancy rates are stationary over time. See Clapp (1993) for a review of natural vacancy rate theory and criticism of the theory.

5   Following the British wartime pattern, rent controls existed until 1981. An important contributing factor to rapid adjustment in rental in Hong Kong is the custom of short lease contracts, a response to legislation that increases tenants' rights if leases are longer than three years. This phenomenon increases both supply and demand of rental properties at any time, and thus increases rental transaction volumes and market efficiency.

4 VALUATION AND DYNAMICS OF HOUSING PRICES (QUADRANT 2)

The price formation process for real estate assets includes at least two interrelated activities. Firstly, when viewed strictly as an investment good from the investor's viewpoint, the value (and price, if the asset is transacted) in an efficient market for real estate assets is a function of the expected, discounted net income (that the real estate asset is expected to generate) adjusted for risk in comparison with alternative investment opportunities. Shifts in investor expectation within the real estate industry as well as changing macroeconomic conditions in the wider economy affect the value of housing assets. Secondly, real estate asset prices in all sectors, including prices for housing assets, also adjust according to the demand for user-ownership (or owner-occupation). Prices for housing assets are therefore very strongly, but not exclusively, influenced by interacting activities of investors who purchase housing assets for the returns they generate on the one hand (investment demand); and those households that choose to purchase their housing units and so secure their flow of services (owner-occupier demand). We address these issues in this chapter, and in particular four questions:

- What are the main factors affecting asset valuation and housing prices?
- How volatile have housing prices been?
- What is the impact of Hong Kong's open economy on prices?
- Could the 1990–1994 housing price escalation in Hong Kong be considered an asset bubble?

The analysis below shows that the behaviour of housing prices in Hong Kong since the early 1980s has been determined by three main factors: one endogenous to the sector and two exogenous to it. The endogenous factor is the growth rate of rents as already discussed in Chapter 3. The first exogenous factor is the nominal interest rate level that is imported from the United States via the Linked Exchange Rate System. This monetary instrument has a very strong impact on the user cost of capital housing.

The second exogenous factor is not a price but a quantity factor. It is the magnitude and direction of net capital flows in Hong Kong.

Similar to the conclusion drawn for the rental market in Chapter 3, the price adjustment mechanism in the market for private residential housing in Hong Kong is shown to be extremely efficient, without significant lags in price changes following changes in expectation. We view this largely as the outcome of clear and stable public policies towards the sector, although this clarity and stability has been somewhat affected by policymakers in 1994. In early 1997 the underlying causes of the 1994 interventions still prevailed, and calls for further intervention from politicians and home-ownership interest groups were heard as house prices once again rose substantially. This chapter aims to provide theoretical background for the interpretation of housing asset price movements in Hong Kong, and we draw the conclusion that some of the concerns surrounding the market for housing assets are indeed real — but in sum the market in Hong Kong does provide adequate mechanisms to adjust for these through the price mechanism and existing financial regulatory institutions and forbearance.

Financing Costs, Expectation and Real Estate Asset Valuation

The total demand for housing units is a function of household formation and other demographic considerations, accumulation of wealth, income growth, in a society generally, and more, and in a particular market segment. In a market with private ownership, the total stock of units will be divided between the two classes of asset owners (who could of course also be mobile between the two activities). In order to indicate how these two different classes of housing asset ownership interact in Hong Kong, we discuss first the theoretical considerations that inform price formation for *investment demand* and then the theoretical consideration that inform price formation for *owner-occupier demand*; and then we point out that the two groups behaved consistently with theory over the period of analysis.

Investment Demand

As stated, demand for housing assets can broadly be divided into two categories (and so can the demand be divided for all real estate assets), namely investor demand and owner-occupier demand. As investment goods, the level of rent **R** earned by real estate assets directly affects their attractiveness and therefore influences directly the process of asset price formation (**P**) in the market for housing investment. We know that the level of rents is determined in the rental market, and that investors purchase a current and future income stream. The analysis of the demand for ownership of real estate assets is illustrated in Figure 4.1.

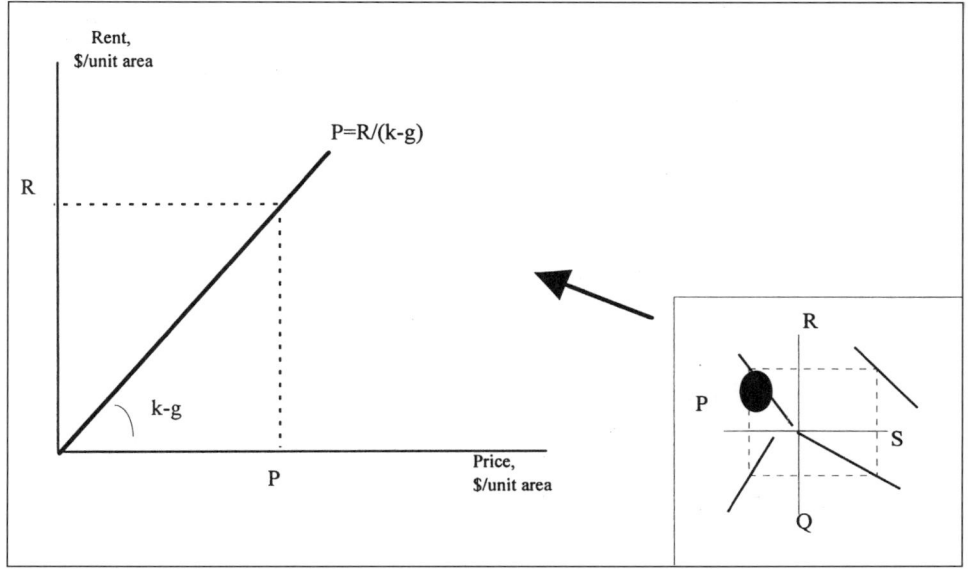

Figure 4.1　Quadrant 2 — The Determination of Asset Prices (Mirrored Image of Second Quadrant)

In order to model the behaviour of real estate investors, the FDW approach depicted in Quadrant 2 relies on the familiar Constant Growth Dividend Discount Model (DDM),[1] one of a family of discounted cash flow models aimed at valuing investment goods. This is an extremely useful and robust analytical tool, which enjoys widespread use and acceptance in real estate markets everywhere, including Hong Kong.

The Constant Growth DDM as an asset valuation model does not assume a particular investment holding period,[2] and is of the form:

$$P_o = \frac{R_1}{k - g} \tag{4.1}$$

where P_o represents the price at the present time ($t = 0$); R_1 represents the net rental income at $t = 1$;[3] g represents expected growth rate in rent, the mechanism through which expected future capital gain is included in price movements;[4] and k represents investors' risk-adjusted target rate of return.[5] When applied to real estate investments, Equation 1 is frequently used in the following manipulated form:

$$k_o = \frac{R_o}{P_o} + g \tag{4.2}$$

where $\frac{R_o}{P_o}$ represents the 'current yield' of the asset.

The 'current yield' has two important functions in real estate investment decision-making. Firstly, it is employed as a benchmark to compare different properties that have entered the sales market, both with one another *and* to what would be observed current yields in a market at a time. This gives an indication of the relative attractiveness of different investment opportunities at a time without reference to price. 'Observed current yields in a market' are generally derived from a representative sample of most recent market transactions.

Secondly, current yields are also used to estimate asset values at a time and hence bid/ask prices. Because Equation 2 can be rewritten as $\frac{R}{P} = k - g$ observed current yields (or individual investors' target current yields) can be used in Equation 1 as a 'capitalization rate' (or income multiplier),[6] i.e. the rate at which **R** is capitalized to estimate the asset's value (which is assumed for the present to equal its price).[7] Current yields are also frequently referred to as 'initial yields' and 'rental income yields'. Current yields and their movements provide extremely important insight into market activities and investor behaviour at any particular time and is one of the most closely watched real estate variables in all sectors of the Hong Kong real estate market.

Current yields in a market result from four considerations: long-term interest rates in the economy (which in large measure determine mortgage interest rates); the risks associated with investing in real estate; the expected rental income growth; and tax considerations. It is represented by the slope of the ray emanating from the origin of Quadrant 2 (see Figure 4.1). We follow convention that current yields represent a benchmark used by investors to evaluate the bid/ask prices of assets.

A reduction in required current yields, caused for example by increased expectation (+ g) with the same overall target rate of return (k) would cause the ray to rotate clockwise and prices to increase despite static rental income (see Figure 4.2). Similarly, an increase in current yields, caused for example by decreased expectation (– g) or perhaps an increase in long term interest rates (+ i) or the risk of the asset class, would cause the ray to rotate counterclockwise and prices to decrease despite static rental income and unchanged rental growth expectation. In this way we see changes in property prices, despite there being no change in rental income generated by the properties.

Figure 4.3 presents a time-series on total (unlevered) returns earned on housing investment in Hong Kong from 1980 and also returns from current rental yields over the same period. This shows that although investors in residential real estate may have earned relatively low rental yields, their total returns have been extremely high when capital gain over the period 1984–1994 is included. From Figure 4.4, it also seems clear that the negative relationship between capitalization rates and price movements suggested by Equation 1 holds in Hong Kong. Changes in required initial yields translate through the capitalization of rentals into price changes in assets, although the direction of causation cannot be clearly determined from these observations.

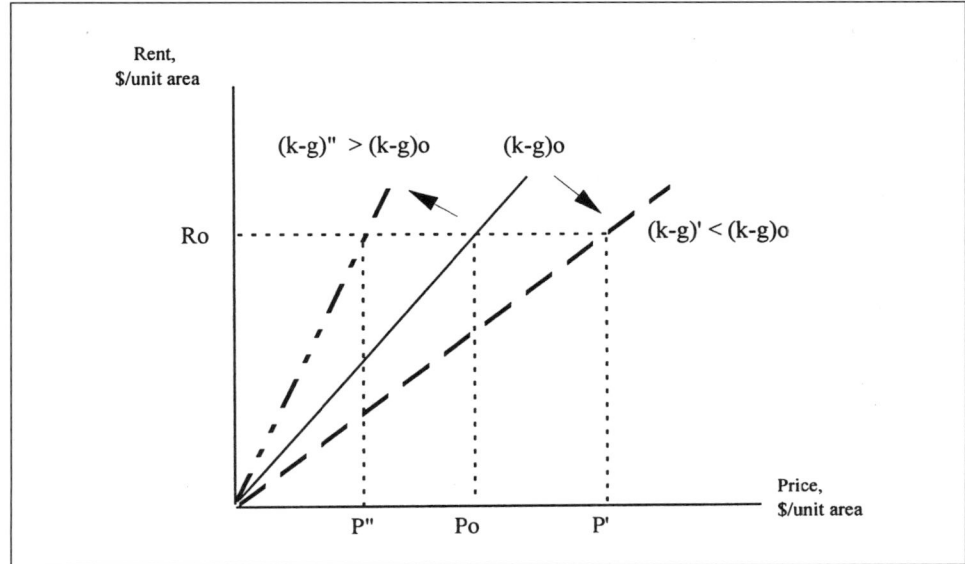

Figure 4.2 Effect of Changes in Capitalization Rates on Asset Prices

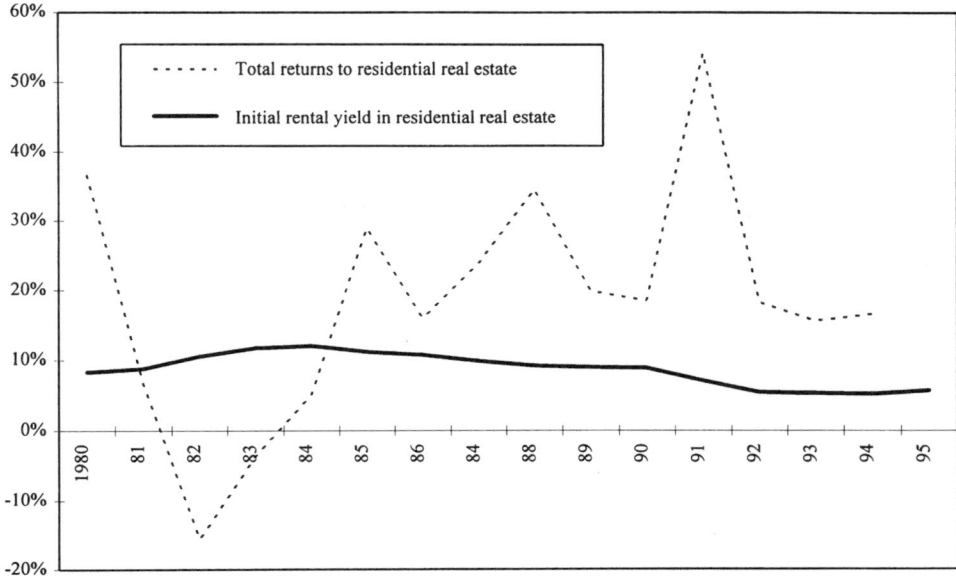

Sources: Rating and Valuation Department, Hong Kong government; K.W. Chau, Department of Real Estate and Construction, The University of Hong Kong (for total return series).

Figure 4.3 Total Returns and Initial Rental Yields to Residential Real Estate

1979 4th qtr = 100

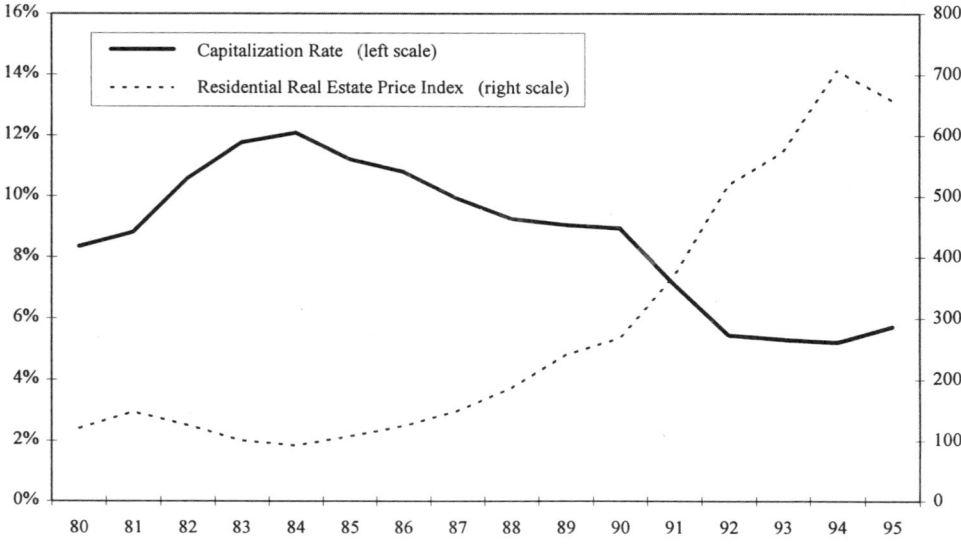

Figure 4.4 Capitalization Rates and Real Estate Asset Prices

At this stage it is also useful to point out that as national and local economies mature, real estate investors generally expect a lesser proportion of total returns to derive from capital gains and more from rental income yields. But in Hong Kong, we still have the seemingly contradictory situation that an increase in initial rental yields are actually viewed with some alarm, because it generally indicates that prices are decreasing — and therefore that total returns are under downward pressure. This is exacerbated by the Hong Kong market convention of quoting and reporting sales transactions in price per unit area rather than yields, a convention that is very useful in a market with fairly homogeneous stock. Nevertheless, despite a moderation in economic growth over the last few years, the principal component of total real estate returns in Hong Kong has continued to originate from capital gains which emphasizes the continued strong influence of growth expectation in Hong Kong. The nature of capital gain as a principal source of total returns therefore makes asset price movements of utmost importance to investors, and in turn the very high observed capital gains from investing in residential real estate clearly would also have influenced households to purchase their housing in order to capture these gains as owner-occupiers; particularly as these gains can be substantially improved with financial leverage.

Owner-occupiers

The above analysis focuses on investment in housing assets in Hong Kong over the period 1980–95 from an investor's viewpoint. It pointed out that the very big proportion of returns derived from house price increases as a component of total returns earned. The principal proportion of private housing assets in Hong Kong are owner-occupied (around 75%), which introduces tenure preferences (renting versus buying) as an influencing factor in housing asset price movements. This leads us to introduce a complementary analysis of different indicators that are more revealing of the capital market forces affecting housing prices in Hong Kong than capitalization rates, although the two approaches rest on the same theoretical foundations. For internal consistency, the FDW model also allows reconciliation of asset price movements with owner-occupation behaviour (DiPasquale and Wheaton, 1996). The Hong Kong evidence of this process is particularly revealing, and provides evidence that Hong Kong housing market participants are entirely rational in their tenure choices.

In the market for housing assets, investors purchase assets for returns offered by these assets compared to other investment goods. Purchasers of housing as an investment good are in competition for the available assets with users of the flow of housing services provided by the assets. Users of housing services have a tenure choice: owner-occupation or renting.[8] In essence, the decision to owner-occupy therefore combines both investment and consumption decisions. As could be expected, the tenure choice is dependent on the comparative cost of the options to consumers, assuming no other obstacles to market entry such as wealth or other constraints, and the user cost principle allows direct comparison of the cost to the household of renting versus buying. With all else equal, equilibrium in the housing market requires that the user cost of owner-occupation and renting be equal (Pozdena, 1988) which means that the periodized rental price and cost of purchase of the same housing unit should instantly converge. In practice, of course, there is continuous adjustment in relative prices between the two options towards this equilibrium.

The housing user cost of capital, UC, is therefore an important and most useful concept in explaining the effect of tenure choice on prices in housing markets, and, as is demonstrated below, provides crucial insights into housing price movements in Hong Kong particularly over the period of rapid price increases from 1990 to 1994. The demand for housing assets by a given household is a function of several factors: the 'user cost of housing capital', the income of the households, its wealth and expected risk adjusted returns on other assets. The user cost itself can be expressed analytically with various degrees of complexity because it is an adjusted interest rate experienced by a specific owner of a specific housing asset depending on his/her expectation, tax rate and financing arrangements.[9] Asset demand models based on the user cost principle range from very simple to quite complex based on optimization models with an explicit modelling of expectation (Miles, 1994). The simplest formulation of user cost can be shown to be:

$$UC_t = P_t (i - h) \tag{4.3}$$

where the user cost **UC** at time **t** is related to the cost of borrowing **i** and the expected rate of housing price appreciation **h**. In the user cost formulation we therefore substitute the expected rate of *price* appreciation for the expected rate of growth of *rents* (**g**). In a perfect market the two rates would be converging instantly to equality. For a given net user cost that is affordable to the household, the smaller the adjusted interest rate (**i-h**) the higher the price the household will be willing to pay for housing assets. Figure 4.6 shows that the equivalence between rates of rental growth and price appreciation have approximately tracked each other with some major divergence such as the period 1990–94 that requires explanation.

The data series for Figure 4.5 can be divided into four periods: 1980–84, 1985–90, 1991–93, and 1994–95. The annual rates of change in rents and residential prices for each period differ significantly. Table 4.1 shows that both rent changes and expectation have been important factors in housing prices. In particular, nominal rents have been rising rapidly after 1984, the period corresponding with the rapid economic re-integration of Hong Kong and China. Over the longer term housing prices in Hong Kong have been responding to fundamental trends in the demand for housing services. Figure 4.6 shows again the high degree of housing rent and price flexibility in Hong Kong.

Figure 4.5 and Table 4.1 both suggest a pattern of regular overshooting of housing prices beyond rent trends. The process of real estate price discovery in Hong Kong has been investigated by Fu and Lo (1995), who studied the behaviour of stock and real estate prices. Like Barkham and Geltner (1995) found for the US and the UK, Fu and Lo find that prices of Hong Kong real estate stocks traded on the Hong Kong Stock Exchange are leading indicators of real estate prices, but they also find that 'in all the real estate markets, prices overreact to rental changes' and it seems that Hong Kong is no different.

Table 4.1
Housing Rents and Price Changes in Hong Kong, 1980–1995

Annualized Rate	1981–84	1985–90	1990–94Q2	1994Q3–95
dR/R (rents)	4.0%	13.9%	9.9%	9.3%
dP/P (prices)	−4.8%	19.9%	30.2%	1.0%

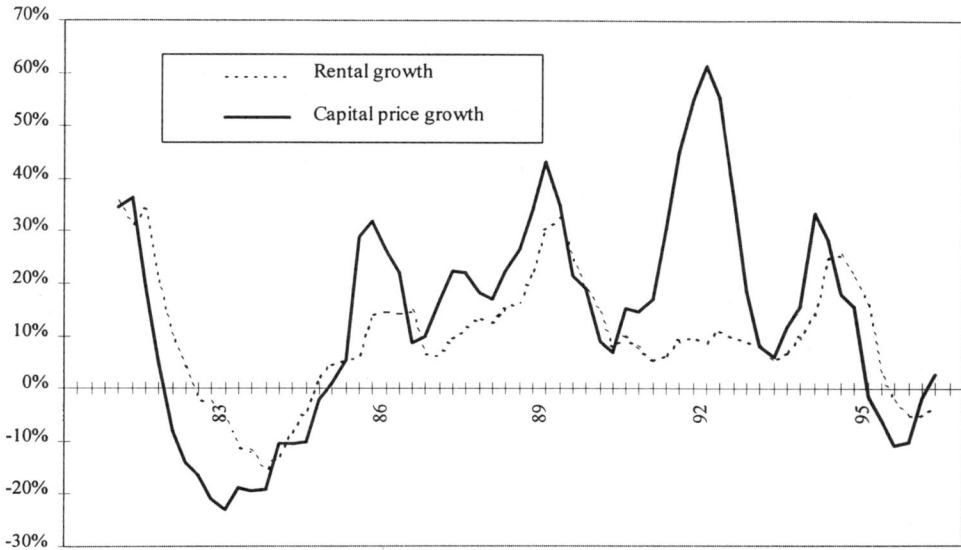

Source: Rating and Valuation Department.

Figure 4.5 *Annualized Price and Rental Changes for Housing, 1981–1995*

Hong Kong's Open Economy and Impact of the Linked Exchange Rate System

In order to understand the behaviour of interest rates and its effect on the user cost of housing capital and thus real estate prices in Hong Kong, it is essential to understand Hong Kong's exchange rate regime, the Linked Exchange Rate System. The LERS is the anchor of Hong Kong's open economy and its single most important macroeconomic instrument.[10] This monetary mechanism influences every aspect of economic life including real estate and other non-traded goods. Its continuation is central to the continuation of Hong Kong's economic system and its success. The Hong Kong Dollars is fixed officially at around HK$7.8 to the US dollars, and through free currency trading and convertibility, interest and currency arbitrage between the Hong Kong and the US currencies, the LERS functions to maintain the fixed exchange rate. Since October 1983, the LERS has provided Hong Kong with exchange rate stability (see Figure 4.6). The practical implication of the LERS is that as benchmark Hong Kong imports United States interest rate levels which are not necessarily appropriate to its domestic inflationary environment. Between 1988 and 1994, inflation in Hong Kong remained consistently below the banks' Best Lending Rate (prime rate), implying large negative real deposit rates (see Figure 4.7).

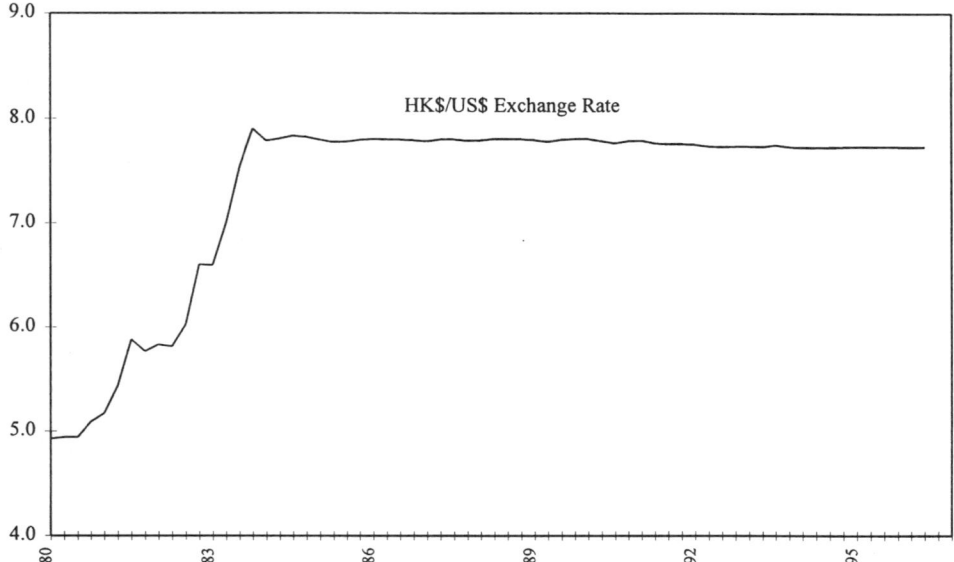

Source: Hong Kong Monthly Digest of Statistics.

Figure 4.6 The Hong Kong Dollar Exchange Rate

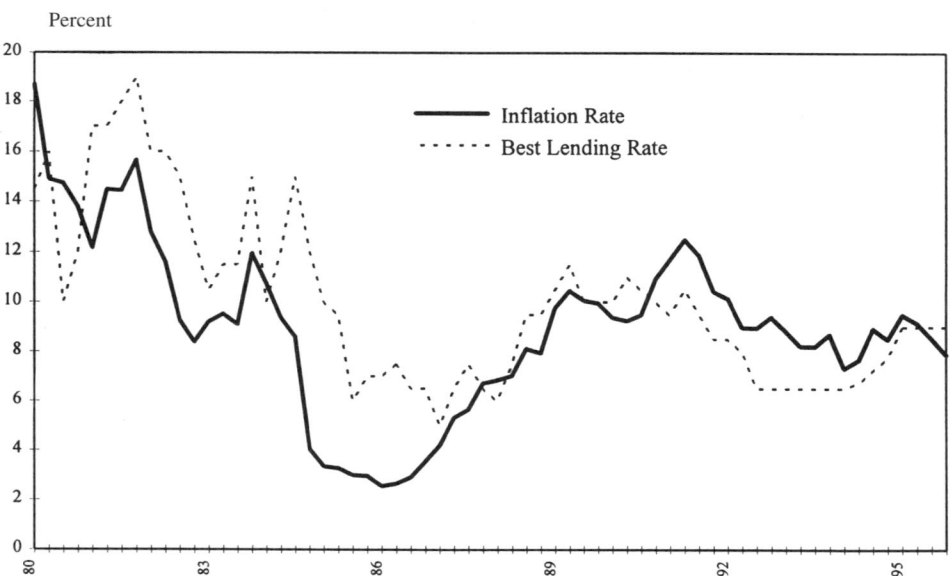

Source: Hong Kong Monthly Digest of Statistics.

Figure 4.7 Best Lending Rate and Inflation Rate

As Figure 4.5 has shown earlier, changes in rent and capital prices have largely behaved in a consistent manner from 1981 to 1990 reflecting endogenous conditions in the housing sector. A break appears in 1991, precisely at the time when the Hong Kong real estate market experienced negative real interest rates, inflation was higher than the Best Lending Rate and large capital inflows from China occurred.

Ex-Post User Cost of Housing Capital and Housing Prices

We proposed above that observing investor behaviour alone in the market for residential real estate was not very useful to explain housing price trends. On the other hand, the simple aggregate indicator of the user cost of housing capital experienced by Hong Kong investors is extremely effective in explaining the behaviour of housing prices. A comparison of the rent and price behaviour (presented in Figure 4.5) with quarterly variations in the user cost of housing capital simply measured as the difference between the mortgage lending rate and the rate of housing price appreciation **i-h** (presented in Figure 4.8) indicates the power of the user cost **UC** in explaining both positive and negative changes in the rate of housing price appreciation.

Figure 4.8 indicates that the user cost of housing capital was generally negative for the period from around 1986 up to 1994 and sharply negative between 1991 and

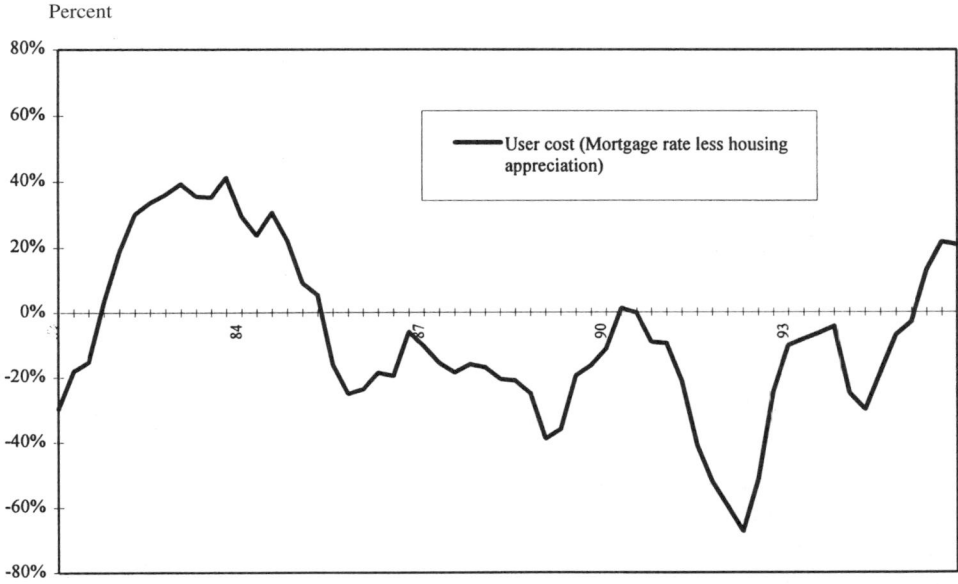

Source of data: Hong Kong Annual Digest of Statistics.

Figure 4.8 Simple Measure of Net User Cost of Housing Capital, 1981–1995

1994, until interest rate movements in the US prompted an increase in mortgage rates in Hong Kong. Negative user cost effectively means that it is profitable to own housing, thus creating a high demand for assets, and with supply lagging for structural reasons (see Chapter 5) it resulted in rapid asset price inflation over this period. Other factors such as the structure of demand for housing services and assets also came into play, and are elaborated in Chapter 6. In addition, trading geared assets in a liquid market with increasing prices clearly became an extremely attractive activity, as indicated by the transactions volume over this period.

Once mortgage interest rates increased and the user cost of capital became positive in April 1994, prices predictably stabilized and even came down. This coincided with two other phenomena that acted to reduce prices, namely the level of credit risk concentration in the banking sector (see 'Concluding Remarks' on page 63) and government action to reduce real estate prices in the face of political pressure (see Chapter 8). It would appear if government action at that time exacerbated downward price movements that were already taking place within the market mechanism.

Impact of External Capital Flows on Housing and Other Real Asset Prices

The sharp appreciation in housing prices during 1991–93 goes beyond the range suggested by the user cost values for the period. This episode needs additional explanation. During that period, massive capital inflows from China poured into the Hong Kong real estate market. It is estimated that as much as HK$15 billion poured directly into the Hong Kong real estate market in 1991 and 1992 from China alone (Hastings and Li, 1996). Additional flows poured in from the US as a result of low US domestic rates of return through portfolio investment into the Hong Kong stock market that is itself dominated by real estate stocks. Figure 4.9 illustrates Hong Kong's estimated net external capital flows as a percentage of GDP between 1981 and 1994, indicating net positive inflows over 1991–94 at the same time as rapid housing price increases occurred.

Impact of the Rate of Appreciation on Asset Trading Volumes

There is usually a positive correlation between the rate of appreciation of an asset and the volume of trading in that asset. Figure 4.10 presents monthly volumes of sales and purchase agreements and confirms this dynamic in Hong Kong. Such trading volumes should be compared to the typical monthly volume of completed (private) units which has rarely risen above 3000 new units per month (see further discussion in Chapters 5 and 6). Figure 4.10 shows four distinct periods which correspond

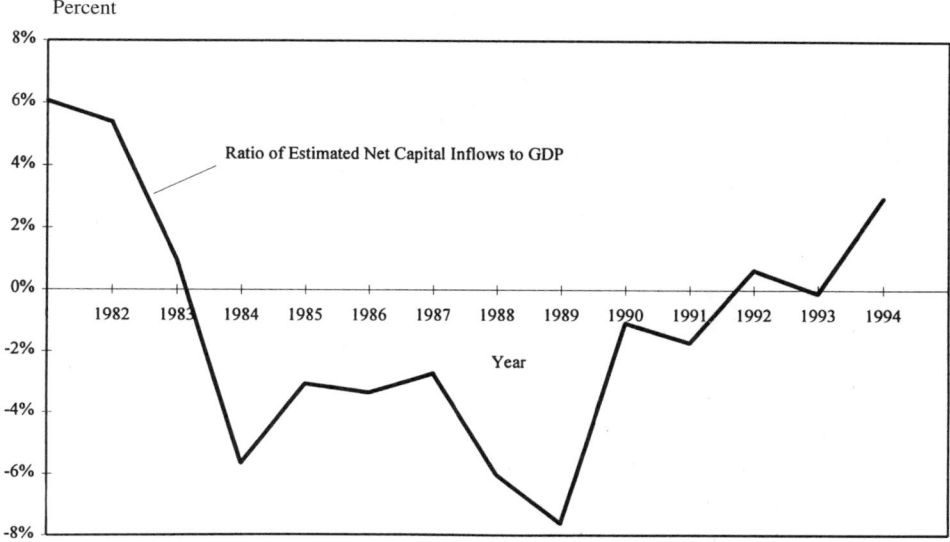

Sources: Hong Kong Monetary Authority; Census and Statistics Department.

Figure 4.9   Hong Kong's Estimated Net External Capital Flows (% of GDP), 1981–1994

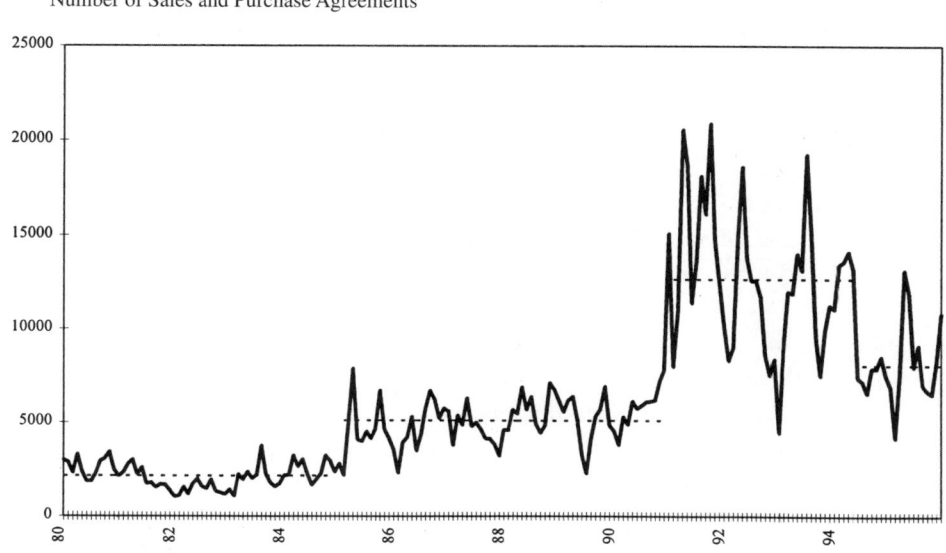

Source: Land Registry.

Figure 4.10   Monthly Real Estate Transactions Activity, 1980–1995

directly to the rates of price appreciation (dP/P) that were reported earlier in Table 4.1.

- Period 1980–84 was characterized by a serious bank crisis and real estate asset price deflation in 1981–1982, and uncertainties in the run-up of the Sino-British negotiations on the future of Hong Kong. This uncertainty was checked to a very large extent by the introduction of the LERS in 1983. Then confidence was further improved by the adoption of the Sino-British Joint Declaration in 1984. During the period, the volume of transactions fell below the normal level of output of new units.

- Period 1985–1990 shows a level of trading consistent with the typical level of production of new units by the industry. Rents and prices increased gradually and interest rates were above inflation. This period could be labelled 'normal'.

- Period 1991–93 is characterized by the negative real interest rate environment occasioned by the decision by the Federal Reserve Board of the United States to lower interest rates drastically, leading to negative real interest rates in Hong Kong. Trading volumes are several orders of magnitude larger than actual output. In addition to pure trading, a factor of unknown magnitude in this data is the relative importance of 'purchase agreements' or presales which are used by developers to prefinance the construction of new units (see Chang and Ward, 1993).

- Period 1994–95 shows a cooling-down following the reversal in interest rate trends in the US in early 1994. It also reflects the effect of the restrictive monetary policies pursued by China to slow inflation that same year. Both factors contributed to the reversal of external net capital flows for Hong Kong as shown earlier in Figure 4.9. In addition, during this period the effect of the government's 1994 anti-speculation policy measures (including restrictions on presale agreements — see 'Mortgage Lending and Anti-Speculation Measures' on page 60 and Chapter 7) as well as banks' restraint in lending to the real estate sector (see 'Concluding Remarks' and Chapter 7) began to take effect. It appeared that several crucial variables all turned at the same time against further rapid price appreciation.

Following the downturn precipitated by the increase in interest rates in 1994, housing price levels declined by as much as 20% towards the end of 1995, and increased by early 1997 to approximately the peak levels experienced in 1994 (see Figure 3.6). This generated further calls for intervention in the market as fears of another price spiral surfaced. In addition to explaining the nature of the measures taken in 1994 to curb speculation and rapid asset price inflation, an analysis of the 1994 anti-speculation measures provide insights into the nature of options available to policymakers, given the constraints that persist particularly on the supply-side of the market for housing assets (these constraints are also extensively elaborated in Chapters 5 and 6).

The Effect of Presales on the Investment Environment

Asset price behaviour in Hong Kong has been affected very strongly by the extensive selling (and subsequent trading in a quasi-forward delivery market) of housing units before completion. Presales refer to a developer selling a residential unit in a development prior to completion of the unit, frequently under conditions allowing the buyer to pay the purchase amount over the period from purchase to completion.

One of the critical constraints on entry into both the owner-occupation and investment housing market is the purchasers equity (downpayment) required in the purchase of housing units. For Hong Kong, Fu (1995) categorizes this barrier principally as a liquidity constraint rather than an income constraint on households that wish to owner-occupy, based on the high absolute amounts required to overcome the equity constraints to ownership. This high equity constraint is particularly relevant in the secondary market. The current conservative stance of banks, which generally seems to follow the loan-to-valuation ratios of 70% that have been proposed in 1991 by the predecessor to the Hong Kong Monetary Aurthority (HKMA), means that a very sizable equity component frequently has to be secured by potential buyers from sources other than bank loans. Table 4.2 further indicates the magnitude of this barrier, where it is demonstrated that banks have indeed followed increasingly conservative loan-to-value ratios in this decade in the small- to medium-sized flat market, and have been conservative in the extreme in the large flat sector.

It is in this light that the advantage of the presales system on the market for housing assets is better appreciated. Specifically, the presales system affects purchasing behaviour by lowering the equity requirement, because under the presales system buyers are frequently required to give a much lower initial downpayment to secure

Table 4.2
Average Loan to Valuation Ratios, 1994

Period	Small to Medium Flats	Luxurious Flats
1989	88.3%	86.8%
1990	88.5%	87.1%
1991	75.9%	72.9%
1992	72.2%	69.5%
1993	70.8%	64.6%
Sept 1994	69.5%	54.8%

Source: HKMA (1996b), Survey on Residential Mortgages in Hong Kong

the transaction than is the case in the secondary market. There is often a further provision that the amount that should be covered by equity could be paid over a protracted period. For example, given a 70% loan-to-valuation ratio, it is not uncommon that a small percentage (say 10%) is paid as deposit, with the remaining 20% of the equity paid in increments until the completion stage of the development.

Presales could affect investment behaviour both at the time of purchase and at the choice of timing for sale of the real estate asset. Firstly, the lower downpayment translates to lower barriers to entry into the real estate ownership market. Since new supply is usually marketed through presales, the number of potential buyers per housing unit is much higher in the primary market than in the secondary market. Thus, entry into the real estate market is better achieved through the primary market where advantages of lower downpayment requirements and protracted payment terms are available. In this sense, housing units in the secondary market may have been comparatively less attractive because the obstacle presented by the loan-to-valuation ratio becomes a critical factor for many households.

There were likewise low exit barriers in the presales market. This was particularly true until 1994 when the resale restriction on pre-sold uncompleted units was not yet enforced. In a buoyant housing market, as Hong Kong has been for much of the last fifteen years, the steady increases in prices could be an attractive incentive for investors to speculate in the pre-sold housing market, particularly if returns could be geared to the extent that presale agreements allowed. It is commonly believed, in fact, that much of the speculation in the housing market was concentrated mostly in the primary market, due significantly to the advantages provided by the presales system. Presales thus provided a more affordable entry into the market on the one hand (if the balance of equity is raised in the available time) while on the other hand it provides the purchaser the opportunity of capturing interim capital gains if the presale contract had to be disposed of if the balance of equity could not be raised.

The presales system, therefore, also acted to increase demand for assets through the low barriers to entry and to exit in the housing market, and possibly contributed significantly to upward pressure on prices. However, the exact effect of presales on price formation remains debatable, and requires in-depth empirical research.

Mortgage Lending and Anti-Speculation Measures

Memory of the 1983–86 instability in Hong Kong's banking system, and the role that real estate lending played in it, have not faded from banks or regulators' memories. It is therefore not surprising that an issue raised by the high rate of asset appreciation during the years 1991–1993 and the ballooning volume of trading was whether inappropriate bank lending was a significant factor in housing asset price inflation.

The evidence presented on the rapid growth of real demand for services as well as the impact of US interest rates, negative local deposit rates and capital inflows suggests that the impact of bank lending was relatively marginal to the situation. Whereas regulatory concerns about the structure of lending are made clear to banks, banks have generally also been prudent in guarding against credit risk concentration in the real estate sector. An important example of this occurred in early 1994, when aggregate lending to the real estate sector in Hong Kong exceeded 40% of total lending (see Figure 4.11), a proportion considered to be a prudent upper limit by the HKMA (1994b). At the end of 1993, around 37% of total lending to real estate (approximately 16% of total lending in Hong Kong) was for real estate development and investment, with the balance of lending generally financing residential mortgages for owner-occupiers. If it is kept in mind that residential mortgages are almost exclusively originated in the banking sector in Hong Kong (with a small proportion originated by developers as part of their sales strategies), the credit risk exposure of the financial system and how it might affect future lending to households has caused some concern at that time.

Individual banks' exposure to the real estate sector obviously are obscured by these aggregates. However, lenders that were faced with high sectoral credit risk concentration clearly acted to manage their own exposure by prudent lending policies, as in clear from Figure 4.11 and Figure 4.12. Aggregate measures of mortgage portfolio variables indicate that as aggregate lending to real estate increased, the spread of mortgage rates over Best Lending Rate progressively increased, the ratio of mortgage instalment payment to borrower income exhibited a slight decline, and maximum loan to valuation ratios declined substantially. Banks clearly have been aware and have acted on their exposure to the residential real estate sector.

Yet anti-speculation measures were introduced in 1991 in the form of recommending to banks that they observe a ceiling of 70% on loan-to-value ratios (which recommendation was maintained until the present) and in 1994 it was recommended that debt-service to gross household income ratios of 50% should be used in new lending to residential real estate. The 1994 measures only seemed to accompany the reversal in price pressures already in progress, following the 1991 efforts to curb speculation. As far as the financial system was concerned, the measures implemented were mostly prudential in nature and aimed to improve the safety and soundness of the banking system despite the fact that the quality of the residential mortgage portfolio as of September 1994 was very good. At that time loans to owner-occupiers were 96.5% and the average outstanding loan-to-valuation ratio was 53.3%. Most loans were floating rate loans with an average spread of 129 basis points over the Best Lending Rate, and the amount of default/delinquent loans was less that 0.5% of the total outstanding loans with the four largest banks commanding a market share of about 85% of residential mortgage lending.

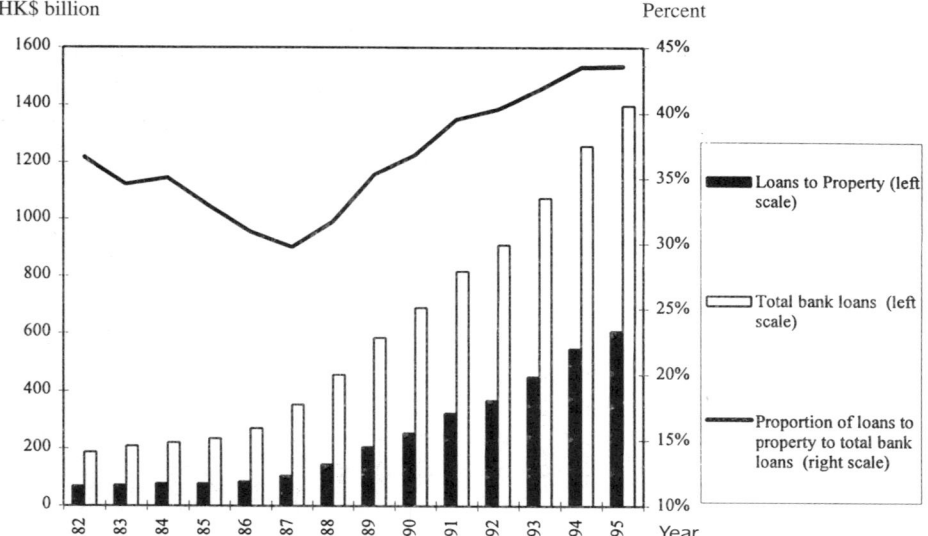

Source: Hong Kong Monthly Digest of Statistics.

Figure 4.11 Share of Real Estate Loans in Bank Portfolios, 1982–1995

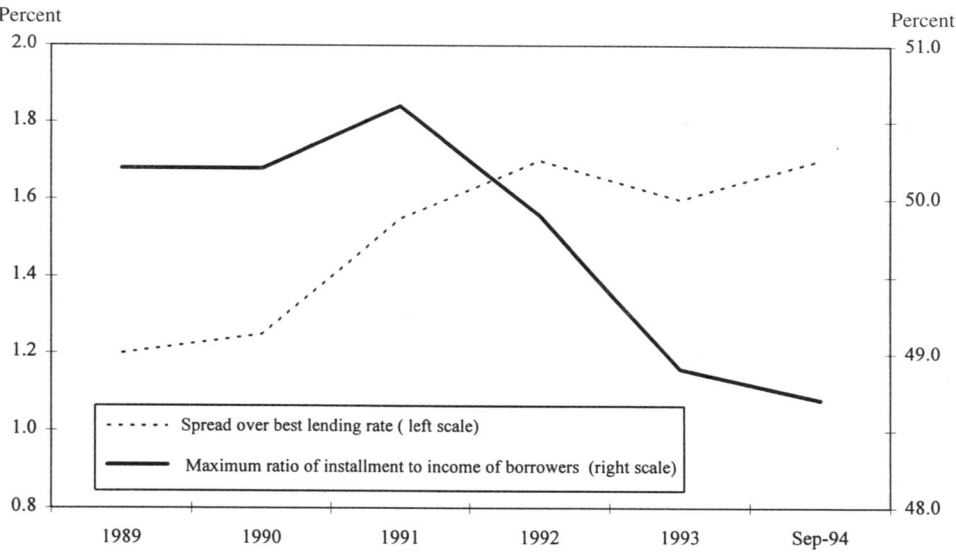

Source: Hong Kong Monetary Authority (1994c).

Figure 4.12 Aggregate Indicators of Hong Kong Banks' Lending Policies to Real Estate, 1989–1994

In spite of the quality of this portfolio, the Hong Kong banking sector was perceived by regulators to have a long-term structural problem with the high share of residential and non-residential real estate loans in their portfolio (see Figure 4.11). The mortgage corporation proposed in April 1996 will be a tool towards better risk diversification, and is considered in more detail in Chapter 7. At the time of writing, the volume of residential mortgages granted had increased over 1994 and 1995 amidst a minor mortgage war between lending institutions in the first half of 1996, but evidence to analyse this empirically is not yet available. In early 1997, the HKMA again resorted to moral suasion by requesting banks to observe loan-to-value ratios of 60% when providing finance to borrowers for the purchase of luxury residences in the territory.

Concluding Remarks

This chapter concentrated on housing asset price formation, and showed that there were high returns to both investment in housing and owner-occupation of housing in Hong Kong, primarily from high price appreciation over an extended period. The price adjustment mechanism in the market for housing assets is shown to be extremely flexible, and responds to fundamentals in an entirely predictable fashion. Despite this, rapid asset price inflation, particularly between 1991 to 1994, was viewed with increasing alarm by the government, politicians and financial regulators alike for different reasons. Possibly as a result of political pressure, the government introduced a set of anti-speculation measures to arrest rapid asset price inflation, at the same time as increases in interest rates and concerns in the financial sector acted to reduce prices. It would seem that like governments everywhere, the Hong Kong government also lacks appreciation of the extremely complicated issue of timing intervention in market mechanisms. In conclusion, it is possible that the 1994 interventions exacerbated the decline in asset prices that had already started at the time when the anti-speculation measures were announced. The policy lesson to be extracted from this is an old one — interventions might at best have the desired effect, but most probably at the wrong time.

Chapters 3 and 4 have concentrated to a large extent on demand factors in the rental and assets market and how these are translated into asset price behaviour. Chapter 5 will deal with the supply of new residential real estate in Hong Kong.

Notes

1   For real estate assets, 'dividends' are earned from all income generated during the holding period, including the rental income stream. Technically, proceeds from the resale of the asset is normally the final dividend.

2   Although the constant growth DDM assumes a constantly growing dividend income stream

into perpetuity in its theoretical framework, this of course does not in practice mean that investors intend to hold the assets in perpetuity. 'Constant growth' also does not imply investors actually expect that rental income growth will be at the same rate for every year into perpetuity, it merely represents average expected periodic growth.

3 In practice R_0 and R_1 are used interchangeably if no shocks to rental income are expected. We assume therefore for convenience that $R_0 = R_1$.

4 With all else equal, every time there is a change in expectation in the market asset prices change accordingly. Rental growth expectation are influenced by expected demand and supply imbalances in the rental market and in part by inflationary expectation. expectation of course change constantly.

5 **k** reflects the time value of money (**i**) and also the risk (σ) of the particular asset class, in this case real estate. From conventional portfolio theory, we define **k** in its simplest form as follows: $k = i + \sigma$, where **i** is the risk-free return (based in conventional economies on the returns earned on government debt). In Hong Kong, the risk-free return would theoretically be benchmarked by US Treasury debt securities following the linking of Hong Kong's currency to that of the US (see the section, 'Hong Kong's Open economy and Impact of the Linked Exchange Rate System' on p. 53). The constant growth DDM essentially represents the summation of an infinite series of dividends, or **Rs**, growing at an assumed constant rate **g**, and has the prerequisite that k>g (see Sharpe, Alexander and Bailey, 1995). It is also necessary to adjust k for taxation effects, which we shall ignore for the extremely low personal taxation required in Hong Kong and for the favourable tax treatment of investment activities in Hong Kong.

6 The current yield represents a measure of the investor cost of capital for period **t**, and thus is also a flow measure of returns to housing investment for the period **t**. The Constant Growth DDM as expressed in Equation 1 does not attempt to represent a measure of investor cost of capital, rather it is a model that informs decision making based on overall target rates of return and prices in the market at time **t**.

7 In an efficient market, value and price should be identical.

8 For convenience we ignore other housing options.

9 Again, because of the extremely favourable tax regime in Hong Kong we have ignored tax in this discussion. Complex tax regimes generally complicate extensively the actual formulation of user cost at the level of individual purchaser.

10 Jao (1993) stressed at the time of the creation of the Hong Kong Monetary Authority in April 1993 that in modern monetary policy there are three main tools for monetary stability: exchange rate stability, domestic interest rate policy, and the control of monetary aggregates. Only one of these alternative tools can be used. As a small, open economy dependent on trade and international services, Hong Kong decided that there is no alternative to an exclusive focus on external price stability, even at the cost of some demand-driven domestic inflation in the non-traded good sectors such as real estate.

SUPPLY RESPONSE AND REAL ESTATE DEVELOPMENT (QUADRANT 3)

The second part of the real estate capital market models the process of supply of new housing assets, and is represented in Quadrant 3. It considers the combination of various resources required to create new real estate assets, and is concerned with the economics of the development industry and the inputs it deploys; namely land, construction services, economies of scale, project economies and more. It is also concerned with factors that constrain supply and how they affect prices.

Five questions are addressed in this quadrant to indicate the location and shape of the supply curve for Hong Kong:
* How do physical and institutional constraints affect access to land?
* How do these constraints affect the market adjustment process?
* How does access to capital affect the structure of the real estate development industry?
* What is the role of presales in financing and distributing output in Hong Kong?
* How efficient is the construction industry?

In this chapter, we will show the effect of limited supply of land on the development process in Hong Kong, and also comment on how such factor shortages were overcome in the past. The overall impression that emerges from this analysis is that the supply of new housing units — the 'flow' of new supply — is severely constrained by the availability of land for new development. The availability of land for new development (or the shortage, to be more specific) stems primarily from limits placed on the release of land by the government following the 1984 agreements between the British and Chinese negotiators concerning the management of land in Hong Kong during the transition phase.

On the other hand, we also point out the efficiency of the physical delivery of real estate in Hong Kong, given the factor and institutional constraints that exist. The scale at which the top real estate developers in Hong Kong function, and the level of operational efficiency at which they deliver their products is unsurpassed worldwide at the present time. Yet these companies are frequently blamed for collusionary practices, which have made them the target of politicians and sections of the community that have been crowded out in the bidding process following high demand for the limited flow of new housing stock. This bidding process has functioned and continues to function as a rationing mechanism to allocate the restricted flow of new housing stock in Hong Kong, and unfortunately the government, in its steps to arrest the ensuing growth of asset prices, have also affected on occasion the efficiency of these companies.

Supply of New Real Estate Assets

The decision to develop new private residential supply is an entrepreneurial response to price movements caused by activity in the rental and asset markets (Q–1, Q–2). Decisions to develop new space follow favourable expected sales margins over development costs of new assets. Figure 5.1 is a simplified representation of the real estate development and construction industry and its response to current real estate prices. In principle, the amount of new units supplied to the market are dependent on the capital price of the asset in the market P, the price intercept a, and the slope b. In standard fashion, the quantity of new construction will be larger when first, the market price is significiantly higher than the fixed cost represented by a; second, the entry cost is lower and a is smaller; and third, the slope of supply curve b is large.

A simplified representation of price and supply of new construction can be given by the relationship:

$$Q = \frac{P - a}{b}$$

which indicates that the amount of new real estate assets supplied in the market is dependent on the capital price of the asset in the market, P; the price intercept, a; and the slope, b. In particular, the quantity of new construction will increase as: (1) the market price is significantly higher than the fixed cost; (2) the fixed cost decreases; and (3) the slope of the price-new supply curve decreases. The slope of the variable b, on the other hand, can here be taken to be affected by the efficiency of the construction industry, as well as the market efficiency provided by institutional arrangements and custom affecting allocational and transactions efficiency in a real estate market.

In principle, these variables illustrate effectively the conceptual divisions between the development industry and the construction industry. The intercept a is a function of land scarcity and other structural constraints and prevailing institutions, and leads to prevailing land prices in a market for land. This in turn suggests a possible range

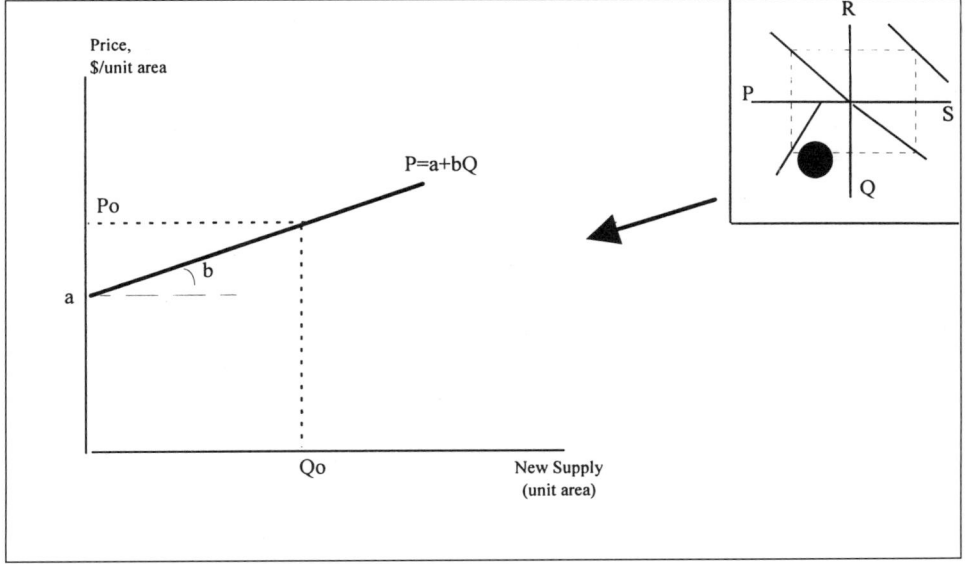

Figure 5.1 Quadrant 3 — The Supply of New Residential Real Estate (Inverted Image of Third Quadrant)

of factor combinations to overcome the constraints. In turn, the construction industry through competition provides economically efficient technical solutions to physical product delivery and so influences the slope of the supply curve **b**. Housing price elasticity of supply is therefore affected by the efficiency of the construction industry, as well as the efficiency provided by institutional arrangements and customs affecting allocational and transactions efficiency in a real estate market.

Access to Land: High Entry Costs and High Density Multipurpose Development

The real estate industry in Hong Kong is directly dependent on one dominant factor — land supply. Access to land is the critical factor for commercial success in real estate development in Hong Kong. While the cost of land represents a basic fixed cost of developing any real estate in market economies at a particular time, at present this cost is extremely high in Hong Kong at between 60% to 80% of total development cost, indicating the scarcity of the factor at the most fundamental level.

At its present stage of political development, Hong Kong has an overall limit on gross land area which, for geographical and political reasons, translates into a physical limit on developable land. Figure 2.1 has provided an indication of the extent of land constraints in Hong Kong. This limited supply of developable land is the direct cause of high residential density in Hong Kong's established urban areas. Probably around 20% of Hong Kong's geographical area is conventionally developable (see Map 2). This leads to high-rise solutions to the land shortage.

Another critical factor is that government essentially has a monopoly over the release of new, previously undeveloped land through the leasehold land tensure system. The land supply policy of the government for many years has been such that it was perennially lower than demand and this has resulted in a high land price environment. Over the years the physical shortage of land has triggered substantial reclamation activities, itself controlled by the Hong Kong government. Annex III of the 1984 Joint Declaration has capped the annual sales of new land leases for all uses (including residential use) to 50 hectares, or about 50% of what total supply has been in the years preceding the Joint Declaration. In addition, Annex III mandates that a 100% conversion tax be applied to the conversion of a lease from its existing to a higher and better use. Figure 5.2 show the sales of new land prior and after the 1984 Joint Declaration.

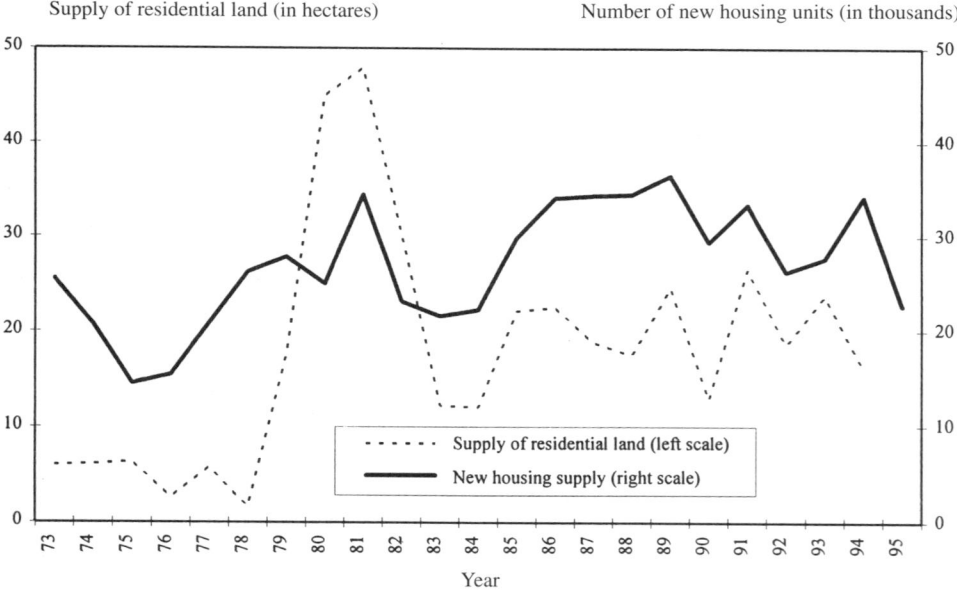

Sources: Land Registry; Rating and Valuation Department.

Figure 5.2 Supply of Residential Land and of New Housing Units in Hong Kong, 1973–1995

The high land cost environment in Hong Kong is, in a sense, an integral part of the territory's fiscal policy. One of the reasons real estate and land prices are high is that real estate also functions as an indirect form of prepaid tax through the sale of

Crown Land leases.[1] Taxation in Hong Kong is low by international standards at 15% for personal income and 16.5% for corporate income. Revenue to the Hong Kong government from the periodic sales of land at high prices has allowed the adoption of lower personal and corporate taxation in Hong Kong, something that would not have been possible had a sizable income source from land and real estate transactions not been available. Public income from real estate transactions over the years has constituted a very high proportion of government income (between one-fourth and one-third). Table 5.1 indicates the relative importance of income generated from land sales to the Hong Kong government. As noted earlier, Hong Kong has been one of the pioneers in the private supply of public services through financially autonomous — and profitable — corporations, which has further reduced direct taxation of individuals and corporations.

Table 5.1
Proportion of Hong Kong Government Revenues Generated
by Property and Land Transactions

Year	Total Revenue	Revenue from property	Share of total revenue	Revenue from land transactions	Share of land revenue to total property revenue
	HK$ Mn	HK$ Mn		HK$ Mn	
1983 – 84	30 400	8 966	29.5%	2 267	25.3%
1984 – 85	36 343	10 880	29.9%	4 268	39.2%
1985 – 86	41 420	12 689	30.6%	5 751	45.3%
1986 – 87	43 870	12 762	29.1%	5 510	43.2%
1987 – 88	55 641	17 035	30.6%	7 702	45.2%
1988 – 89	65 781	29 669	45.1%	15 830	53.4%
1989 – 90	74 365	27 246	36.6%	10 849	39.8%
1990 – 91	82 674	26 610	32.2%	6 618	24.9%
1991 – 92	101 456	41 872	41.3%	21 641	51.7%
1992 – 93	120 781	40 708	33.7%	16 906	41.5%

Source: Walker, et al., p. 52.

There are also endogenous, mostly demand-derived, reasons for high land costs in Hong Kong. Following rapid economic growth, high income growth, and high demand, purchasers of residential units have had high bidding power for the available stock and the flow of new supply for most of the 1980s and the 1990s. In addition, there is continued fierce bid-rent competition from alternative land uses, with a flexible regulatory attitude to zoning changes in Hong Kong. Following the basic residual value function and with a highly competitive contracting industry, this presently translates into high residual values and consequently high prices for any developable land (new or for redevelopment). As an important supplier of this factor through new land release and reclamation, the Hong Kong government's fiscal benefits from land sales is substantial.

The Hong Kong government's land management system operates through a 'contractual zoning system' (Lai, 1996) attached to the leases. In 1956 under the pressure of massive inflows of refugees, the Building Ordinance was modified and plot ratio controls relaxed in a major way permitting much greater substitution between land and buildings.[2] The flexible height restriction on developments further contributes to the high fixed costs of development projects. In order to achieve sufficient gross development income to bid successfully for land against alternative land uses with limited supply of land, developers have to respond by maximizing development scale on the available land. The net result for residential land use of this competition between land uses is supply of a large number of relatively small units in large-scale, comprehensively planned developments, thus substituting for the limited supply of land by increasing the capital content of the structures through high plot ratios while also reducing marginal costs per unit (for modelling of this process, see Peng and Wheaton, 1994).

Apart from allowing higher bid-rent characteristics for the developer, this scale-intensive development provides project scale economies (see Chau, 1995) and through resulting densities also increases the returns to transportation and urban infrastructure investment.

The Effect of Land Constraints on the Market Adjustment Process

As has been discussed, the considerable land constraints in Hong Kong could be traced to the size and topography of Hong Kong, the government's role as the sole supplier of new developable land, and the introduction of the 50-hectare limit on the amount of land that could be released each year for real estate development. The constraints on the supply as a consequence of the constraints on available land for development has an important consequence on the adjustment process in the real estate market. In order to appreciate the effect of supply constraints on the market adjustment process in Hong Kong, it would first be instructive to discuss how the adjustment process works in markets with no constraints in either demand for or supply of real estate. This is done in two ways: first, through a discussion of the relative positions of the supply and demand cycles over time, and second, through a discussion on the cycle of vacancy rates. The analysis presented below is intended to offer additional insights into market behaviour during the adjustment of both demand and supply that would be predicted by the FDW model, but it does not form part of the model per se.

In markets with no significant supply constraints, there are essentially two phenomena in the operation of real estate demand and supply cycles. The first is the lag in the supply cycle during periods of economic expansion brought about by the production lag inherent in the development process, as well as the relative slowness of the development sector in reacting to positive signals of increased demand in the market. The second major phenomenon is the relative volatility of additions to the aggregate stock of space over typical supply cycles when compared to typical changes in aggregate demand over demand cycles, frequently resulting in oversupplied markets. The effect of these two characteristics is that in general during economic expansion it is demand that dominates supply (a consequence of the supply lag) and conversely, during economic downturns, it is supply that dominates demand (a consequence of lumpy assets and the tendency towards overbuilding). In other words, there is typically an alternating dominance of demand and supply — with demand dominant during the expansion and supply dominant during the contraction phases of real estate cycles (see Figure 5.3a).

The behaviour of demand and supply cycles are reflected in the vacancy rates, and thus the consideration of the vacancy adjustment process provides an important alternative way of analysing the operation of the cycles that operate in the real estate market. Central to the understanding of the vacancy adjustment process is the concept of the natural vacancy rate, which is taken to be the level of vacancy at which there would be no pressure for rental levels to change (see Smith, 1987 and Clapp, 1993). In general, rents increase when the actual vacancy rate goes below the natural vacancy rate, while they decrease when actual rents are in excess of the natural vacancy rate. During expansion, when demand for space dominates supply, the vacancy rate tends to decline as additional space is absorbed; while during the contraction stage, with supply dominating demand, net additions to aggregate supply increases the level of vacancy in the market. This results in a cyclical adjustment in the vacancy level (Figure 5.3b), reflecting the cycles in the demand and supply of real estate. It follows from this that the analyses of demand/supply cycles of real estate and the corresponding cycle that may result in the levels of vacancy are complementary and would best be viewed in combination. This is presented in Figures 5.3a and 5.3b, which should be interpreted together.

The complementarity of the analysis of cycles and that of vacancy rates is enhanced when one considers that the process of adjustment in vacancy levels is another source of the lag in the supply following increased demand. This is because at the trough of the real estate cycle when there is excess space, initial increases in demand are manifested first in the adjustment in the vacancy rate through absorption of excess supply and only later through rental and price levels. Following natural vacancy rate theory, upward adjustments in rents occur once the actual vacancy rate is either equal or less than the natural vacancy rate. Increases in supply come much later and occur

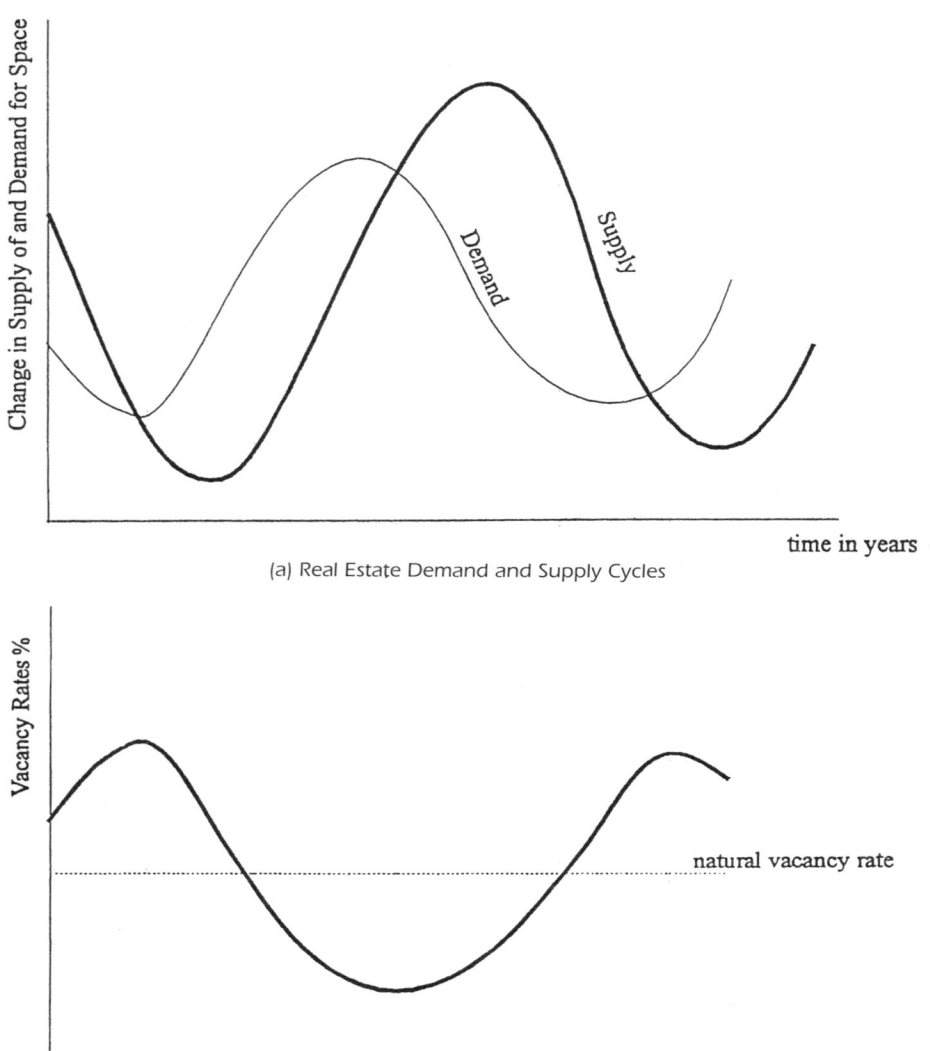

(a) Real Estate Demand and Supply Cycles

(b) Cycle of Vacancy Adjustment

Figure 5.3a and 5.3b Cycles of Demand and Supply and Vacancy Adjustment in Markets with No Supply Constraints

as a consequence of significant increases in the levels of rents and prices. Therefore, the lag in the supply cycle could be partly attributed to the time it takes for the excess vacancies to be absorbed and the equilibrium vacancy rate to be reached.

Overbuilding in real estate markets, on the other hand, could be attributed to the lumpy nature of real estate assets and the time required for the physical production and bringing to market of real estate units. Traditionally, there are two underlying factors that are considered to be the principal reasons for overbuilding: (1) myopic behaviour of developers in bringing supply to the market all at the same time, and (2) the practice of non-recourse lending by banks.[3]

One of the main points of this discussion is that the real estate supply cycle would be quite different in markets with significant supply constraints such as Hong Kong. In the first place, the fact that there is inelastic land supply generally means that there is limited or no overbuilding in the market, leading to a supply cycle that is less volatile than the demand cycle (see Figure 5.4a). While there would still be a lag in the supply cycle, this lag could be expected to be much shorter due to the shorter vacancy adjustment process. The absence of overbuilding considerably reduces the supply volatility in the market. This may result in a situation whereby the actual vacancy rate more often is lower than the natural vacancy rate or, if greater, it is generally much closer to the natural vacancy rate (see Figure 5.4b). The relative absence of supply factors in the adjustment process suggests that rents and prices would be much more responsive to changing market demand conditions.

This analysis provides fundamental insights into the reasons why real estate markets in Hong Kong seemed to have escaped the crippling effects of overbuilding that regularly affect markets with fewer factor constraints. Four reasons are offered for Hong Kong's good fortune. First, there is the physical constraint of developable land in Hong Kong due to the smallness of its territory and more particularly to its topography, as has been pointed out. Second, the government exerts important control over the supply of new land made available for development. In this capacity as supplier of land, the government can influence the timing and magnitude of land made available for real estate development in Hong Kong significantly, and indeed has a financial interest in doing so. Third, since 1984, there has in any event been a limit placed on the allowable amount of land that could be released for development following the Joint Declaration. Fourth, limited availability of land force developers to engage in the practice of 'land banking' to secure efficient supply of developable land for future activities, thus emphasizing the importance of access to land as barrier to entry. Landbanking is a long-run strategy; and thus the myopic behaviour usually attributed to developers elsewhere generally cannot be attributed to Hong Kong developers. The concept 'developers' myopic behaviour' in fact presumes that there are no constraints on land supply. Land banking suggests that developers have a long-term plan to utilize their land banks in such a way as to ensure that they have

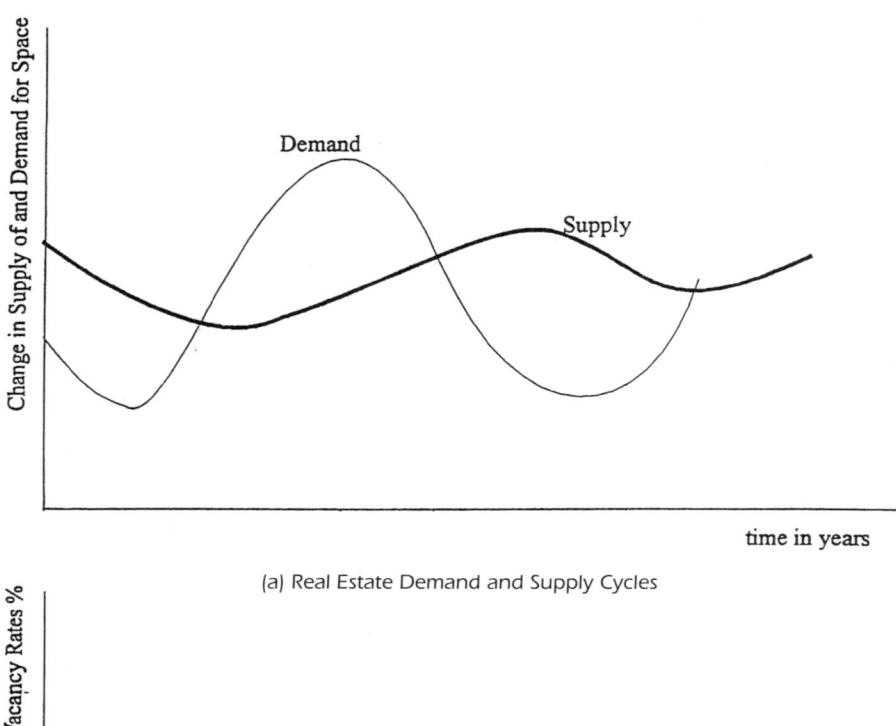

(a) Real Estate Demand and Supply Cycles

(b) Cycle of Vacancy Adjustment

Figures 5.4a and 5.4b Cycles of Demand and Supply and Vacancy Adjustment in Markets with Significant Supply Constraints

steady development opportunities over time. This in itself has a moderating influence on supply.

The absence of overbuilding in Hong Kong has important implications for the adjustment process. During an overbuilt phase, the vacancy rate reaches its highest level. The higher the vacancy rate, the longer it will take for the excess vacancies to be absorbed; the path from peak vacancy to equilibrium vacancy would therefore be much longer. An absence of overbuilding suggests that at any given time, the actual vacancy rate is closer to the equilibrium vacancy rate. Rent therefore adjusts much faster to changing demand conditions inasmuch as the excess vacancies would be absorbed much faster. This explanation corroborates the point stressed in Chapter 3 which described the high demand elasticity of rents in the Hong Kong real estate market. (See 'Rent Flexibility and Hong Kong's Natural Vacancy Rate' on page 38.)

We have seen that in markets with no constraints there is alternating dominance by demand and supply. For such markets, this is essential to the adjustment process. Increases in demand results, after a lag, in increases in rents and prices which in turn provide the incentive for supply to increase. The resulting increase in supply dampens the tendency of rents and prices to increase further, and in this sense is an important steadying factor in the adjustment process because it generates critical market information. The land constraint that characterizes the Hong Kong real estate sector disrupts this adjustment process. With severe restrictions in land supply, increases in

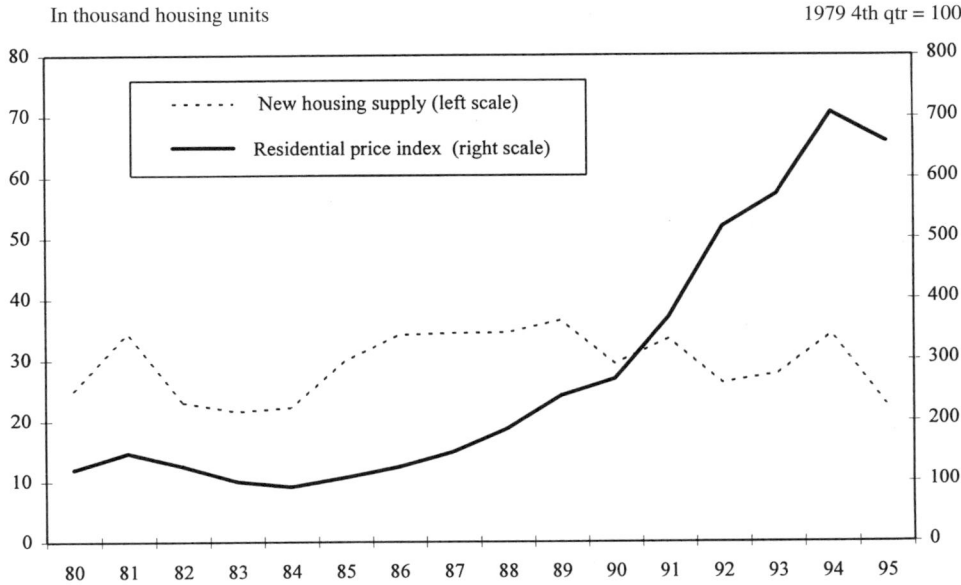

Figure 5.5 New Housing Supply and Housing Price Movements

rents and prices due to increases in demand may not be matched by an increase in supply. If supply remains flat while demand continues to be buoyant (albeit possibly cyclical), a relative undersupply situation results which puts pressure on rents and prices to increase further. This could even be regarded as structural undersupply, and could be gleaned from Figure 5.5 which shows a relatively constant net addition to housing stock despite the impressive appreciation of the prices of housing units during the last few years. It would seem, therefore, that the market adjustment process in Hong Kong is characterized by the inability of supply to match demand and this perception would clearly have important consequences for expectation in the market. With supply unable to keep up with demand, the upward pressure on prices caused by excess demand might be taken to be a permanent condition. Speculative activities in the market in Hong Kong could very well be due to the market's anticipation that increases in demand would not be checked by a corresponding increase in supply.

Captial, Large-Scale Developments and Structure of the Real Estate Industry

What characterizes Hong Kong apart from other real estate economies is that the technology and organization utilized in the development and construction process is essentially the same across the various land uses, namely high-rise scale-intensive projects with a high technology content and capital-intensive supply processes. This is of course substantially different from economies where land supply is not as constrained, thus allowing more industry fragmentation and a variety in delivery processes and project scales. As already noted, Hong Kong is one of the important world models of high density urban development.

High project costs (see Figure 5.6) and a limited supply of land necessitate access to large capital resources and a high liquidity position for acquiring land at short notice without unacceptable financial risk, which to a great extent explains the domination of real estate development in Hong Kong by large and vertically integrated corporations. As an indication of their sheer size, the market capitalization of Sun Hung Kai Properties, Cheung Kong Holdings, Henderson Land development and New World Development, the top four real estate development companies in Hong Kong, exceeds US$ 62 billion (calculated from *International Businessweek*, 8 July 1996). Real estate development companies of this size lose the project-dominated nature that characterizes real estate development in North America, Europe and elsewhere; and start resembling continuous operation enterprises like manufacturers or trading companies. Given their size and continuous demand for developable land, the developers' response to land access problems is good access to capital. Developers in Hong Kong need to have and indeed have excellent business relationships with the

HK$ million at current prices

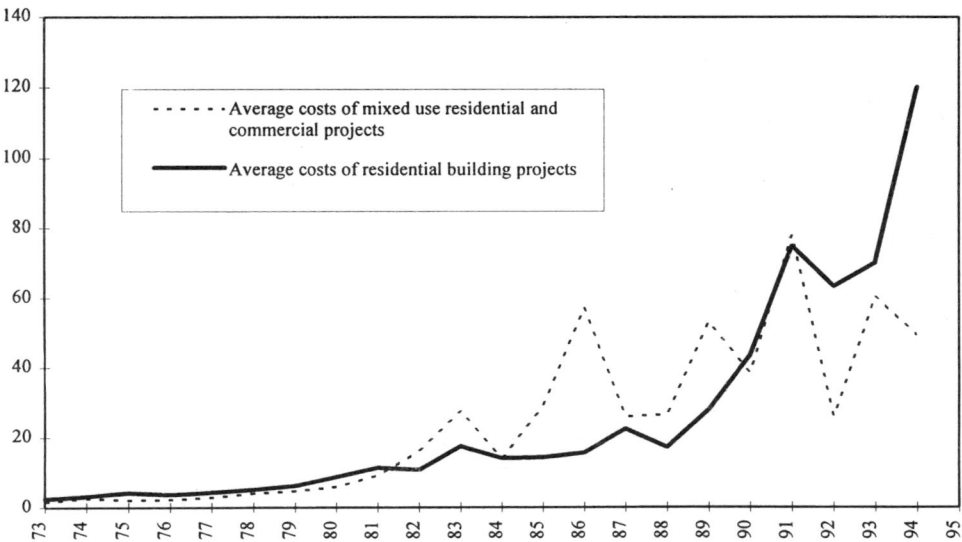

Figure 5.6 *Average Project Costs for Mixed Use and Residential Projects, 1973–1995*

financial community. This allows them financial flexibility to secure at short notice suitable developable land for future development, which may also partly explain why Hong Kong developers maintain conservative financial structures and generally seem to be cash-rich.

As mentioned, real estate development in Hong Kong is presently dominated by very large, vertically integrated and highly capitalized companies that rely on the financial sector for working capital and the Hong Kong Stock Exchange for equity capital. Pure development vehicles comparable to Limited Partnerships in the United States and other forms of financial participation in developments are largely absent. Joint ventures between landowners and small- and medium-scale developers have been common and exhibit great ingenuity, but are declining as redevelopable land becomes more scarce and more expensive. Working capital requirements are still mostly through conventional limited or non-recourse credit forms similar to acquire, develop, construct loans with properties as collateral. There are no real estate investment trusts in Hong Kong and legislative barriers to these investment and financing vehicles are under investigation, as mentioned earlier. A limited number of outstanding mortgage-backed securities issues exist in Hong Kong, but the influence of providers of capital to the real estate sector outside the equity market and the banking system is marginal. It is quite noticeable that the skills developed for various types of urban projects by the major development companies in Hong Kong are currently applied across Asia, also in infrastructure development projects.

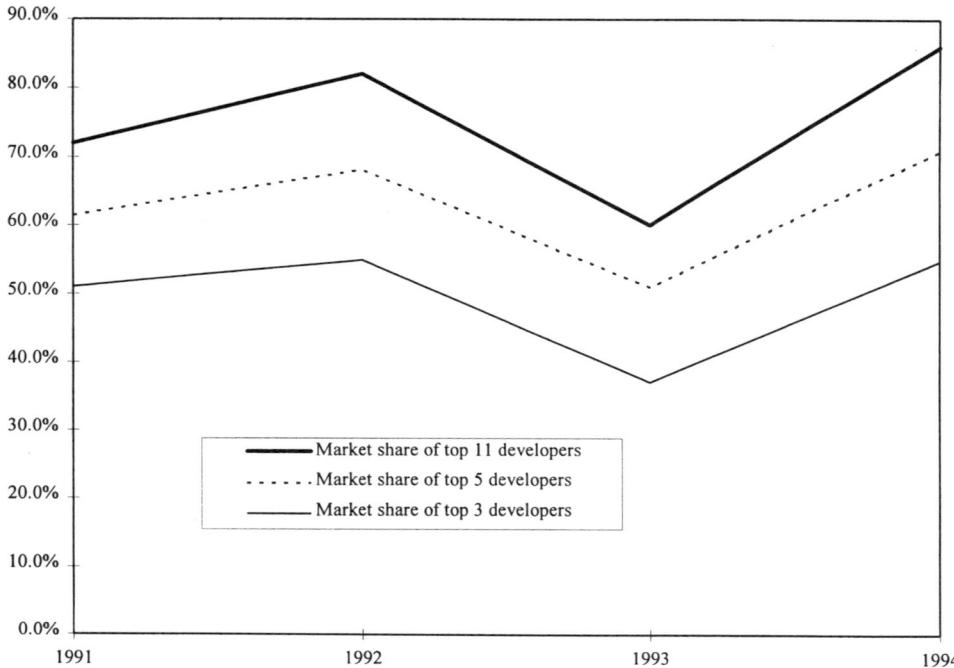

Source: The Consumer Council of Hong Kong, 1996.

Figure 5.7 *Market Concentration of the Development Industry in Hong Kong*

The basic structure of the development industry in Hong Kong is presented in Figure 5.7. Although an aggregate presentation that covers new housing supply, all major developers are mobile and active across land uses and we therefore believe it is representative for real estate development generally. It indicates a high level of concentration, with approximately eleven companies accounting for 75% of industry turnover in the period 1991–1994, and a high 86% in 1994.

The presence of a number of very large, well-capitalized corporations in the market competing for land results in smaller developers simply not being in a financially competitive position to bid on large tracts of land, without taking imprudent financial risks. The ability of larger developers to bid for bigger site areas likewise allows them to develop mixed-use properties in prime locations with substantial positive internalized economies such as shared modern facilities. Most final users are typically willing to pay higher prices for units in a large and comprehensively planned development with considerable internal economies and amenities. It is because the total development environment and development 'neighbourhood' can be more effectively planned and designed with project scale (see Lai, 1996). The ability to develop at scale and internalize the consumer preferences so derived is a further advantage that sets large developers aside from small developers, who routinely have to rely on redevelopment opportunities and discontinuous business circumstances associated therewith.

The large-scale nature of development projects in Hong Kong thus favours established developers and could explain the concentration of big firms in the real estate development industry. This concentration in the industry will persist because the considerable barriers to growth in the real estate development sector keep increasing the pressure towards concentration. The fairly long cycles in the real estate market likewise works towards industry concentration because correct decisions made at a particular point of the real estate market cycle can give a developer a huge advantage to build a large market share that will be difficult for others to challenge until the next real estate cycle (Wong, 1993). But it is nevertheless important to point out that such a share can only be defended with continued supply of good land — which requires high capitalization and liquidity.

High Flexibility of the Construction Sector

It can be argued that marginal cost as a proportion of overall cost of producing new real estate assets in Hong Kong will change very little, as it is unlikely that supply will become less scale-intensive or process-intensive as long as land supply restrictions remain; and while supply at scale continues to provide sufficient economies to bid successfully against competing land uses. If this is so, then the slope of the construction supply curve in Hong Kong could be considered to be relatively flat. This suggests that the amount of new units supplied is affected most by the price intercept which is for the most part affected by land prices. Construction cost, meanwhile, typically accounts for only 20–40% of overall development cost even at the scale-intensity of projects in Hong Kong.

Previous research provides some analytical insight into supply responses in Hong Kong. The first formal estimate of the supply elasticity for private housing in Hong Kong is by Peng (1993), who finds that the price elasticity of supply is no less than in the United States (Peng and Wheaton, 1994). This is a remarkable result given the severe physical constraints that apply in Hong Kong, and it derives from the Building Ordinance which has permitted a high rate of substitution between building inputs (high plot ratios) *and* the high efficiency of the construction industry.

The combination of a high aggregate rate of investment, an open economy with free capital flows, international procurement and tendering, and a very sound and extremely flexible contracting environment has led to high rates of innovation in all sectors. In many economies, the construction industry is perceived as a lagging sector of low productivity growth, but Chau and Lai (1994) have shown that this is not the case in Hong Kong. While the Hong Kong construction sector remains somewhat more labour-intensive than other activities, its rate of productivity growth has been equal to the high growth of the overall economy during the period 1980–1991.

Efficiencies in the Finance and Distribution of Development Output in Hong Kong

In Chapter 4 (See 'Mortgage Lending and Anti-Speculation Measures' on page 61), the presales system was discussed in relation to the effect it produces on the demand for ownership of housing. In this section, the presales system will be discussed insofar as it impacts on the development sector. For the purpose of this discussion, we have isolated the effect of two characteristics of presales on real estate development in Hong Kong. The first is through its role as an alternative source of development and construction finance, and the second is through its ability to save developers from the costs and risks involved in holding inventories of completed flats upon building completion.

Presale has functioned as a viable source of development and construction finance for developers in Hong Kong. The earlier developers are able to presell their new (as yet uncompleted) inventory, the higher the benefit of this alternative source of development and construction finance. The benefit of this source can further be optimized to the firm when developers are afforded the freedom of choosing the timing of presale of uncompleted units. It is noteworthy that until 1994, the government has placed no constraints on presales, except in ascertaining that the interest of the buying public are protected. Presale consents were usually given upon satisfaction by the developers that the building process is in a relatively advanced stage; this is taken as an assurance that the developers will complete the building and honour presale agreements.

The second benefit of the presales system to developers is its role in reducing the risks of holding completed units that would otherwise be borne by developers. This specifically refers to the practice inherent in the presales system whereby developers are able to conduct internal sale arrangements of some portion of the new supply with selected real estate agents. The internal sale arrangement, from the point of view of developers, transfers the risk of holding the inventory to these agents. The practice of internal sales benefits the developer by relieving them the risk of selecting the right moment to conduct the sale (Wong and Staley, 1992).

The massive project scale at which developers are forced to deliver as a prerequisite for competing in a market with limited access to land introduces serious inventory risks for developers. High-rise development means that incremental additions to the stock could be quite sizable, especially in large-scale mixed-use residential and commercial projects. In the absence of presales, a single development could literally introduce thousands of units into the market at a single time, and force developers to carry the full cost of all units until all are sold. Under less fortunate circumstances, developers would be forced to shoulder the full carrying cost of unsold units. The presale arrangement thus affects the variable cost component of the supply curve because presale and internal sale arrangements provide developers with better working capital management opportunities as well as lower carrying cost of uncompleted units, when compared to the condition where presales are not allowed.

A presumption underlying the internal presales phenomenon may be that developers are less efficient at searching out the highest bid for the units and therefore resort to internal presales as a form of risk-sharing. As shown by Wong and Staley (1992), real estate agents and speculators have a comparative advantage over developers in searching for a prospective buyer for a unit because they are in a better position to adjust the price and the timing of each sale. This advantage allows real estate agents and speculators to be comfortable with bearing more risk than the developer may be willing to. It also means that the price of acquiring a unit from real estate agents and speculators will have to be higher to reward them for the risks they take.

Concluding Remarks

The scale and efficiency of the major real estate development companies in Hong Kong is impressive. Despite being faced with high demand for new stock that structurally appears to outstrip supply (given constraints on the supply of land as a basic input), the industry remains highly competitive and produces with scale economies and very low marginal costs. The profitability of the companies, impressive as this may be, does not allow them the luxury of relaxing — the competition for attractive and developable land is fierce and completes the logic of economics in the pricing of scarce resources: the shortage of land is where high residential prices in Hong Kong originates, and the development companies are merely the converters of this scarce resource into a final product. In policymaking towards the sector, the government have at last started to accept this fundamental principle, and in early 1997 it announced the release of some 250 hectares over the following five years for private residential housing alone.

In summarizing the effect of the above factors on the overall shape of the supply curve of real estate in Hong Kong, the conclusion is that high land cost is the most critical factor affecting the intercept of the supply schedule. This intercept had also been increasing gradually between 1973 and 1988. However, after that date it shifted upward very rapidly: between 1988 and 1994 the average value of a project had increased four-fold in 1990 constant prices (Figure 5.6 is in current prices). On the other hand, the marginal cost of an additonal unit is small and is likely to change little (except with inflationary pressures) with present technology and project scale. Given the existing land supply restrictions, the prospect that supply will become less scale-intensive is remote, and it also indicates that market conditions will continue to favour large developers.

However, whereas the analyses presented here concentrate on new supply and is therefore a flow measure, the principal proportion of total supply on a market at a time is generally drawn from the existing stock of housing assets. This introduces the total stock of housing units and its adjustment as the closing sector of the FDW model.

Notes

1　The land regime based on Crown Land operates in a dualistic way across the territory. On Hong Kong Island and Kowloon, 'land was regularized into land lots which were then allocated as leaseholds to private users by competitive auction or tender and to charities and government departments by grants at nominal costs . . . The land in the New Territories was left intact and "leased back" to the villagers.' (Lai, 1996)

2　The height of a building depends on the permissible plot ratios in turn vary according to the size and location of the land lots. For instance, 'the maximum achievable plot ratios for "Class" residential sites is 15. The exact height of a building depends largely on the site coverage which the "Authorized Person" would like to adopt. A Class C residental block with 100% site coverage can be built to 15 story, 50% to 20 storey, and so forth [...] As plot ratios are not uniformly applied to individual land lots, highly irregular building profiles dominate the cityscape of Hong Kong.' (Lai, 1996: 99)

3　Grenadier (1995) provides a good discussion of these two sources of overbuilding in real estate markets.

6 THE STOCK ADJUSTMENT PROCESS IN HONG KONG (QUADRANT 4)

Analyses of real estate development processes by their nature frequently concentrate on the supply of new real estate (the 'flow' of new supply over time), because it is such an important consideration to the construction industry, several profession and also the manufacturing sector of economies. It is therefore not surprising that the impact of the existing stock and its adjustment on price formation in the rental and asset markets is often underestimated. An important contributing factor is lack of cross-sectional and longitudinal data to estimate depreciation and stock adjustment relationships, particularly since real estate assets have extremely long economic lives.

The questions addressed in this chapter are:

- Is the rate of depreciation of housing — and other real estate assets — accelerating in Hong Kong?
- What has been the impact of rapidly rising income and changes in tastes and preferences?
- What has been the impact of high density development on the stock adjustment process in Hong Kong?

In this chapter, we identify important characteristics of the stock adjustment process for housing assets in Hong Kong. It is pointed out that the rapid growth in household incomes in Hong Kong over a very short time has rendered much older housing stock in Hong Kong obsolete. It can be argued that as far as the flow of housing services from the existing stock is concerned, Hong Kong is a victim of its own spectacular economic success: in part the existing housing stock does not generate the composition of housing services that large parts of the population demands, and this fact is exacerbated by various constraints on supply processes. Furthermore, there also exists severe constraints on the redevelopment of existing obsolete urban structures, thus restricting the release of existing (in many cases underutilized) land for redevelopment. This redevelopment friction has important locational implications

— much of the urban land subject to redevelopment friction is in highly attractive prime urban locations in Kowloon and on Hong Kong Island. At the same time there exists a locational mismatch between where developable land is available in the New Territories and where the massive structural changes in the economy over the last twenty years dictate locational preference to be — in the urban areas. In this chapter we also discuss important responses to these problems.

Stock Adjustment

Quadrant 4 of the FDW model represents the process of adjustment in the total stock of real estate assets in a real estate market, i.e. the replacement of depreciated and/or functionally obsolete assets over time. In equilibrium the rate of replacement will equal the rate of depreciation of stock, and there will be no net addition or reduction in the total stock. When the market experiences oversupply of new assets, it also acts to accelerate the rate at which older stock depreciates, the older stock being in aggregate less functionally efficient than the newer stock. The adjustment process is of course not frictionless. Figure 6.1 presents the process of converting the annual flow of construction Q into a net addition/reduction of the total stock S, represented by dS. dS depends both on the addition of new stock to the total stock and the removal of functionally obsolete and/or depreciated stock over any given period, measured by the depreciation rate d.

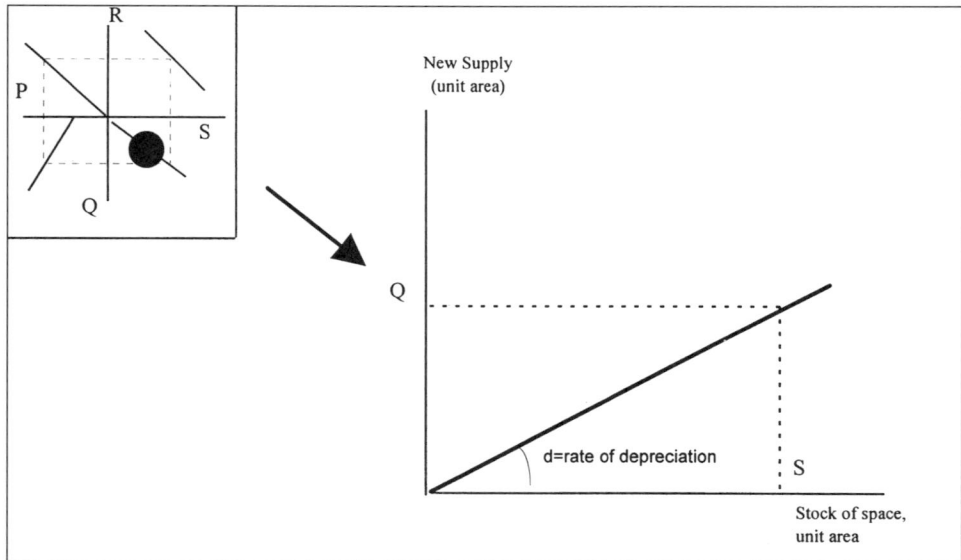

Figure 6.1 Quadrant 4 — The Stock Adjustment Process (Quadrant 4 turned upside-down)

Summarizing the above, the amount by which the total housing stock will adjust in a given period is represented by

$$Q = dS$$

where Q = volume of new construction in equilibrium,
         d = rate of depreciation of existing housing stock,
and S = total supply of private residential stock.

We now turn to particular phenomena in Hong Kong that have and continue to influence the stock adjustment process.

Historically High Rates of Depreciation and Replacement

Over the period 1951–1995, high GDP growth rates and rapid structural change in the economy have also led to substantial structural change in the overall composition of demand for land use in Hong Kong. This in turn has led to a high rate of depreciation of older facilities, processes and structures; particularly, but not exclusively in the non-residential sector. The rate of depreciation of the real estate stock has been very high and the annual rate of economic depreciation of the existing stock probably varies considerably across the five real estate sectors. Unfortunately, no Hong Kong estimates of depreciation rates were identified for this book.

Historically, two regulatory events are considered to have accelerated sharply the rate of replacement of the residential and non-residential real estate stock. First, the 1956 wholesale deregulation of plot-ratios greatly increased the value of all land in higher use and accelerated the removal of old stock. Second, rent control which continued until 1981 had the indirect effect to accelerate the rate of removal of the older, lower grade housing stock (see Ho, 1992 for a general modelling of this process). During the early decades of the post-war period, there was also a high rate of removal of low-cost, low-grade stock, but this process also could not be documented for this book.

Impact of Rapidly Rising Incomes and Changing Household Preferences

It is instructive to provide brief background to the concepts of depreciation of real estate assets in Hong Kong by again referring to Hong Kong's rapid economic expansion over the last five decades. After years of double-digit economic expansion, in 1995 per capita GDP in Hong Kong was estimated to be the fourth highest in the world. In 1995, Hong Kong was described as having the most advanced employment structure of any economy in the world, with some 80% of the labour force employed in services — see Chapter 2 ('High Growth Rates and a Rapidly Changing Economic Base' on page 24). With this expansion also arrived in a very short time a burgeoning middle class with rapidly expanding real incomes. This rapidly expanding middle class demands a totally different bundle of services to flow from residential real estate, and 20-year old residential stock in Hong Kong could indeed be regarded as functionally obsolete. However, this shift does not appear to have taken place yet in the composition of physical stock, and Figure 6.2 shows that the ratio of unit removals from the total private stock has been consistently low and under 0.5% per year. In the United States, where there is a high-income, mature urban economy, this rate has been estimated for housing at 3% per annum (Malpezzi, Ozanne and Thibodeau, 1987). Endogenous forces within the private residential sector may be at work since the rate of supply of new units appears to be of a steady downward secular trend according to Figure 6.2.

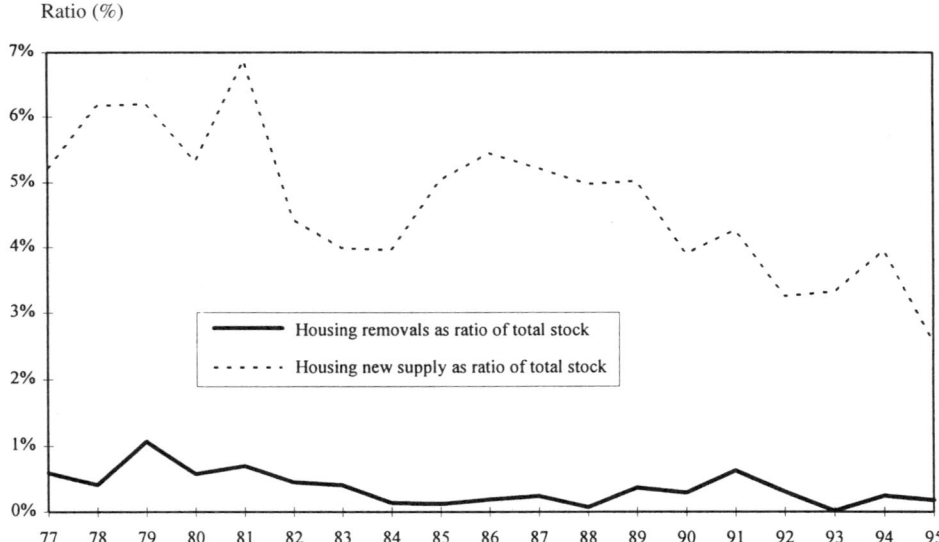

Source: Rating and Valuation Department.

Figure 6.2 *Removal of Old Units and Additions of New Units in Percent of Total Stock, 1977–1995*

As stated above, high GDP growth rates and rapid structural change in the economy have led to structural change in the overall composition of demand for land use in Hong Kong, which in turn led to a high rate of depreciation of older processes, facilities and structures also in the residential sector. Experience in other high density countries like Japan shows that the rate of inventory loss increases rapidly from the moment the market is in 'quantitative balance' i.e. the number of units is equal to the number of potential households.[1] The doubling-up ratio has improved greatly in Hong Kong over the last two decades, but it was still at 1:1.3 potential households to one housing unit in the private sector in 1991. It is equal to one in the public sector which operates outside market rules (Peng, 1993). A more recent figure remains to be estimated.

The private residential real estate sector in Hong Kong is at present and has for the last decade been principally demand-driven. Composition of demand also indicates a shift towards higher demand for space and quality standards. When coupled with a fairly high rate of household formation due to natural demographic factors as well as smaller household size, one can safely assume that a large proportion of the housing stock supplied in the 1950s and 1960s is inappropriate to present demand characteristics and practically obsolete. However, there are several factors that limit the redevelopment of old stock in Hong Kong to adjust to the changing composition of demand. In our opinion, there are a number of factors that deserve to be identified that slow down the redevelopment process down or act to accelerate it. Although several of these factors mentioned are interrelated, we believe it is perhaps useful to outline the factors that act to slow the process down first.

Impact of High Density Development on Stock Adjustment

High density living within single structures in Hong Kong have led to extremely fragmented property ownership rights, and this complicates severely land assembly for redevelopment in addition to introducing very serious development risks. Highly fragmented property right place restrictions on the availability of old stock for redevelopment and increase substantially the transaction costs associated with redevelopment. Fragmentation of ownership creates through sheer numbers of individual interests in a single structure the risk that a small number of owners could delay the negotiation process towards redevelopment by simply refusing to alienate their rights or by seeking unreasonable prices for their interest in the existing structures; particularly when it is kept in mind that the value of the land component in redevelopment of the land into new stock may be as high as 70–80% of the market value of the new units. The negotiation between hugely fragmented individual private interests and developers assembling land for redevelopment has the potential to delay the redevelopment of obsolete structures for years, particularly when developers have already acquired substantial interests in a building. This could effectively be summarized as the most important factor that functions to reduce the rate of stock adjustment in Hong Kong.

On the other hand, several factors associated with increased household wealth in

Hong Kong tend to accelerate the pressure of rendering older stock obsolete. There is an increased desire for amenity, space per unit, an increased awareness of locational differentiation, and the attraction of economies internal to large-scale new developments have been referred to previously. Older stock simply cannot compete with new tastes. Table 6.1 shows clearly that a large proportion of present stock is more than 20 years old and was built when economic circumstances were altogether different from the present. It is fair to assume that much of this stock would be redeveloped under normal bid-rent conditions.

Table 6.1
Estimated Age of Private Residential Flats in Hong Kong (1993)

Estimated Age (years)	Residential Flats (units in 1993)	% of total
1–5	102 927	12.6
6–10	162 635	19.6
11–15	108 705	13.1
15–20	108 170	13.0
21 and over	346 130	41.7
Total stock	828 567	100.0

Source: Daniel Ho, Department of Real Estate and Construction, The University of Hong Kong.

Based on the above analysis, we suggest that estimating a rate of depreciating (d) of stock for Hong Kong is difficult and would require data not readily available. In the United States — a high-income and mature urban economy, this rate has been estimated for housing at 3% per annum (Malpezzi, Ozanne and Thibodeau, 1987). In Hong Kong one can surmise that it could be even higher due to the rapid rate of income growth and technological change in the economy. This annual rate of economic depreciation is in any case much higher than the annual rate of inventory loss. In spite of rapid income growth in Hong Kong, the net annual rate of inventory loss is relatively modest at an estimated 0.42% at the end of the 1980s (Tse, 1994; Peng, 1993). The ratio of annual demolition to new addition is obviously higher and was 9.5% in 1990.

Two government activities counteract the recycling friction associated with land assembly for redevelopment. One is the creation of new land through reclamation, the other the release of previously undeveloped land. However, as noted, the government is restricted in the quantity it can release from these sources to 50 hectares per annum by the Sino-British Joint Declaration of 1984, resulting in a potential supply flow of 30 000 to 40 000 new residential units per annum. The second, and more controversial government initiative has been the creation of the Land Development Corporation (LDC) in 1988. The LDC was mandated by the government to assist in the recycling of urban land. To achieve this objective, it was selectively empowered to set in motion the severe lever of compulsory acquisition. The LDC faced the criticism that it could become a vehicle used by the government (and more conspiratorially, by private developers) to overcome the friction caused by fragmented property right. In practice, the LDC has had some early success in urban areas with high potential gains from redevelopment (for example where high plot ratio gains were allowed in redevelopment of old stock such as Western District), but there appears to be limited interest from the private sector in redeveloping areas where old stock simply needs to be replaced without plot ratio gains (for example in areas such as Mong Kok). Overall, the LDC has attracted substantial media attention and its activities have become somewhat politicized.

Potential Impact of Mortgage Lending Practices

Turnover figures for older stock in the secondary market suggest that the market for these units is not as active as the market for new units. In itself this can be interpreted as an indication of limited demand and obsolescence in keeping with the flow of services that an increasingly affluent society would demand. There is an additional factor that tends to exacerbate this phenomenon and contributes additional pressure to render older stock unattractive. It is likely that banks' financing policy influences the market in older stock. With few exceptions and presumably influenced by factors raised in Chapter 4 (See 'Mortgage Lending and Anti-Speculation Measures' on page 61), banks are reluctant to provide finance for the purchase of housing stock older than twenty years, which would restrict demand for such units and accelerate pressures to sell and so contribute to recycling urban land for redevelopment.

Impact of Locational Preferences on Housing Stock Adjustment

The factors and processes discussed above ignore to a large extent the locational effects of the structure of demand for housing in Hong Kong. Although the density of development in Hong Kong's urban areas and efficient public transport lends itself to the belief that there is accessibility for everyone to everywhere, this is of course incorrect. It is also necessary to emphasize that locational desirability is an important factor in demand in both the rental market and assets market, and that locational obsolescence is in turn also an important factor in economic obsolescence. Fu (1995) points to the mismatch between the locational aspects of demand and supply of housing that has developed between Hong Kong's urban areas and the New Territories,[2] as is illustrated by comparative vacancy rates (see Figure 6.3). He attributes the widening locational mismatch since the late 1980s to a shift in the supply of new residential construction to new towns in the New Territories, while employment opportunities were growing in urban areas. It was pointed out in Chapter 2 ('The Hong Kong Real estate industry' on page 27) that industrial employment has fallen by 50% from some 900 000 workers in 1984 to 450 000 in 1993 (*The Other Hong Kong Report*, 1994). Fu (1995) estimates that while Hong Kong lost some 445 000 manufacturing employment opportunities during the years since 1987, some 580 000 employment opportunities were created in the banking and finance sector alone during the same period. This dramatic changing structure of employment location is the result of Hong Kong's rapidly changing structure of employment from manufacturing to services — with services employment mostly located in urban areas (see Figure 6.4). Fu further points out that this changing locational structure was not accompanied by investments in transport infrastructure, in keeping with the concept of self-contained new towns with local manufacturing dominating new town inhabitants' employment. Overall, mismatches in demand have thus served to increase demand for well-located housing in urban areas of Hong Kong. In turn, this has placed a premium on housing in urban areas (see Figure 6.5).

Percent

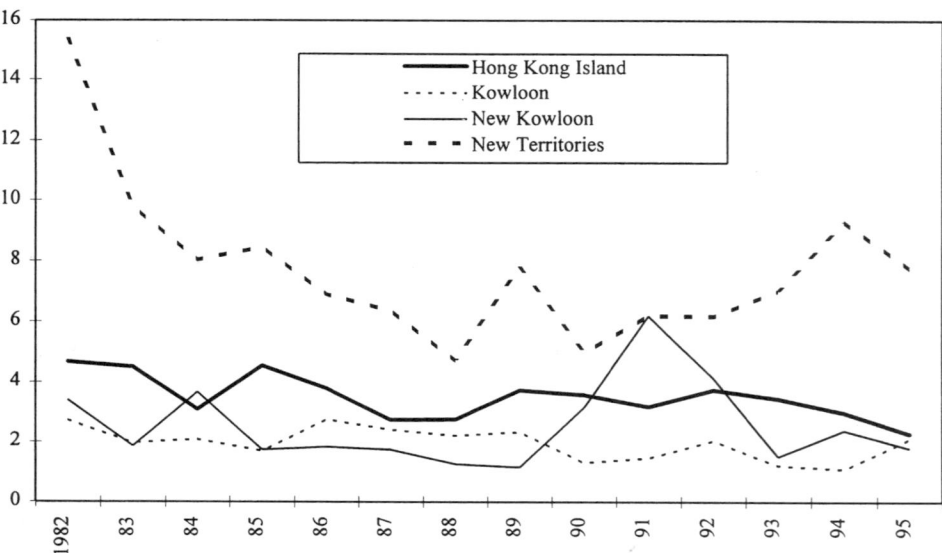

Source: Rating and Valuation Department.

Figure 6.3 Residential Vacancy Rates by Location

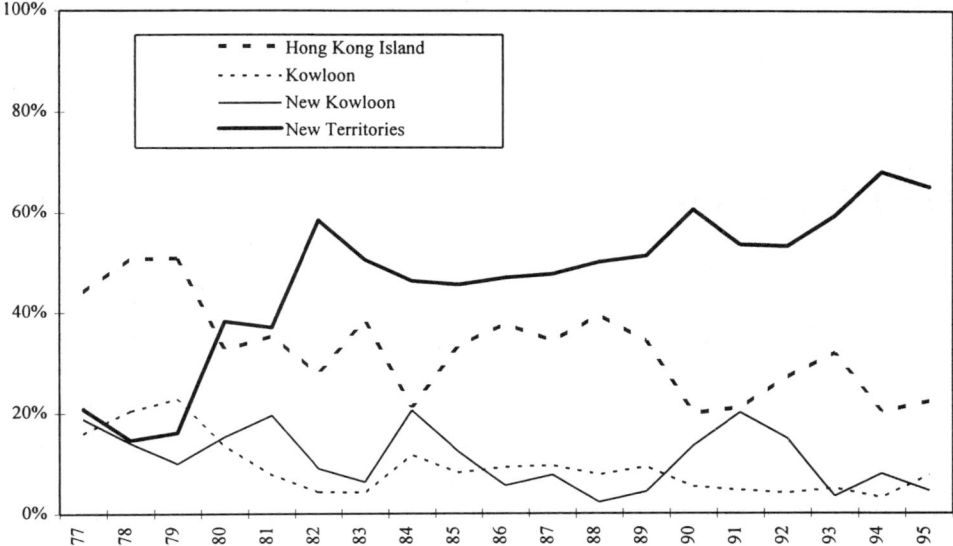

Source: Rating and Valuation Department.

Figure 6.4   Share of New Residential Supply by Location

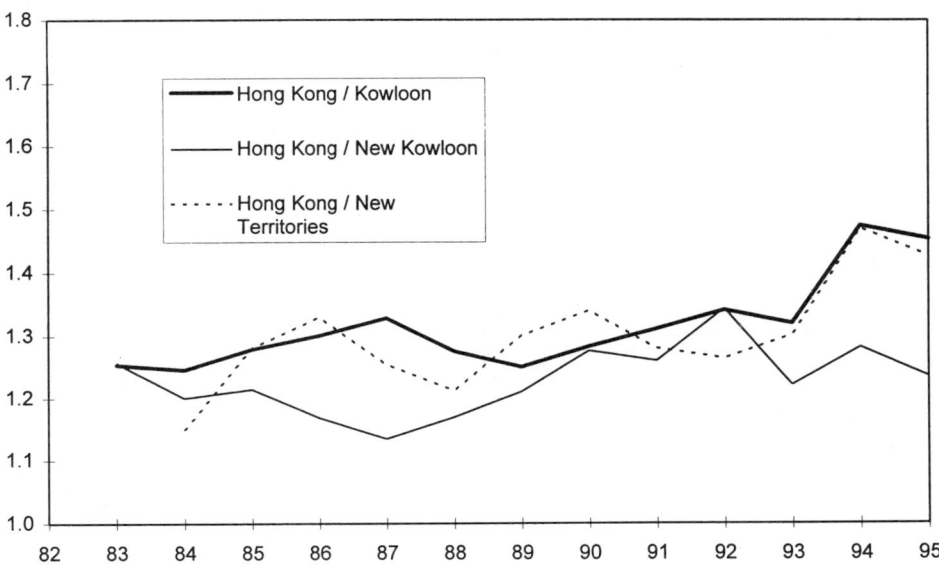

Source: Rating and Valuation Department.

Figure 6.5   Differential Prices of Housing Units by Location

It can be expected that locational imbalances should serve to accelerate further the pressure to redevelop obsolete stock in urban areas, but at the margin the availability of both rental housing and housing for owner-occupation does limit prices in the urban areas.

Concluding Remarks

It has been shown that Hong Kong's rapid economic development and high rates of household income growth have changed the composition of demand for housing services from Hong Kong households, and that the existing housing stock simply does not satisfy this demand. This results in the keen competition for new land supply particularly in attractive locations. As is indicated in Chapter 5, this leads to the rationing of the flow of new supply to those buyers with the highest bidding power. Several problems have also been identified that are inhibiting redevelopment of obsolete stock. In general, it can be argued that in addition to economic obsolescence, much of Hong Kong's housing stock is also unattractively located and may require large investment in transportation infrastructure to become a normal and functionally competitive component of total stock.

The problem of overcoming the friction associated with extremely fragmented property rights over prime land with the existing economically obsolete structures is possibly the greatest policy challenge for the Hong Kong government's land use planning and land management agencies over the next ten years. The economic insights exhibited by the government in bringing about the efficient recycling of obsolete dockyards, industrial land and land freed by relocation of the Hong Kong International Airport is of intense interest to the community. The importance of this scarce resource in an economy based on services cannot be underestimated.

Notes

1   This important sectoral turning point occurred in 1968 in Japan.
2   As a reminder, we follow the definition provided by Hau (1992) in defining Hong Kong's urban areas as the built-up areas of Hong Kong Island, Kowloon, Tsuen Wan and Kwai Chung. This represents about 80 km² and around 60% of the population reside in these areas.

7 USE OF THE FDW MODEL TO INTERPRET POLICY EVENTS

The real estate industry is an important sector in most economies, and inappropriate policy towards it has the potential to cause misallocation of resources on a large scale. In analyses of the various activities that make up the economics of each sector of the real estate markets as modelled by the FDW model, we have identified a limited number of public-policy sensitive characteristics of the structure of the residential real estate market in Hong Kong. We proposed in Chapter 1 that one of the advantages of the two-sector FDW model is that it allows the exploration of particular policy proposals that directly affect the sector, or the possible impact of events in the wider economy that may affect the real estate markets.

In order to test the ability of the FDW model to provide a rigorous framework that could be used to conduct such event studies and assess possible outcomes of policy proposals for Hong Kong, we present in this chapter three analyses based on the insights obtained from studying the economics of the private housing sector of Hong Kong in previous chapters. Firstly, we consider the possible effect on the housing sector in the event that the border between China and the future Hong Kong Special Administrative Region becomes functionally porous. Secondly, we present an analysis of the changes in presale rules that were implemented in 1994 as part of the package of anti-speculation measures of that year. Thirdly, and perhaps more ambitiously, we present an analysis of the housing sector should a present policy initiative, namely the establishment of a Hong Kong Mortgage Corporation, come to fruition. This analysis complements a discussion of aspects of the financial system of Hong Kong that were introduced in Chapter 4.

Our overall conclusion from conducting these analyses is interesting, and possibly predictable. It emphasizes the extremely important influence that restrictions on the supply of land in Hong Kong, irrespective of the causes of such restrictions, continue to exercise in the price mechanism, even with assumed changes in certain structural conditions in the industry. However, we must again caution readers that these analyses are based on our view of the dynamics of the industry, and we do not expect anybody to accept these analyses uncritically — they are merely the outcome of thought-experiments based on our insights described in earlier chapters.

Effects of Opening the Border with China

It has long been a matter of speculation if and how the border between China and Hong Kong will disappear after 1997, together with Hong Kong's political integration with China (see Yeh, 1995). The Basic Law of 1984 stipulates that the border will remain closed and that controls over migration will continue to be enforced as at present. Nevertheless, as is clear from the previous chapters, the most basic constraint in Hong Kong residential real estate is land supply. It is therefore a logical scenario to speculate what might happen if the border disappears or becomes 'porous', allowing sufficient freedom of movement across the border to affect choice of residential location despite place of employment. This could have a marked effect on the real estate market in Hong Kong — land supply would indirectly increase as the adjacent land which is now 'outside' is included.

From analyses presented above, it would seem that the scarcity of land and the various pressures that function to restrict land supply in Hong Kong will continue to shape the supply schedule in short to medium term, in particular the intercept. As long as this is so, the slope of the supply schedule should remain relatively flat with restricted land supply. This in turn translates into high price elasticity of supply — relatively small movements in prices have the potential to earn developers large margins.

If the land supply constraint is removed, for example by integration of Hong Kong with Guangdong province adjacent to Hong Kong, a totally altered supply schedule might result. A massive potential increase in the supply of developable land would result, and this could result in substantially lower fixed costs of development. This would result in a rightward shift of the supply curve as the fixed cost intercept reduces. If the shift is *not* accompanied by a drastic reduction in development project scale intensity (or if there is a change in scale intensity but the magnitude is such that the slope of the supply curve is virtually unaffected), the resulting new equilibrium position is characterized by Figure 7.1.

However, if the shift in the supply curve is accompanied by a change in the scale-intensive nature of development in Hong Kong and brings about a reduction in scale intensity, there will be a corresponding increase in the slope of the supply curve. This could come about if the reduction in land cost was such that there would be no need to resort to high-rise residential developments in order to secure acceptable profits from development activity. With much reduced land cost, the share of construction

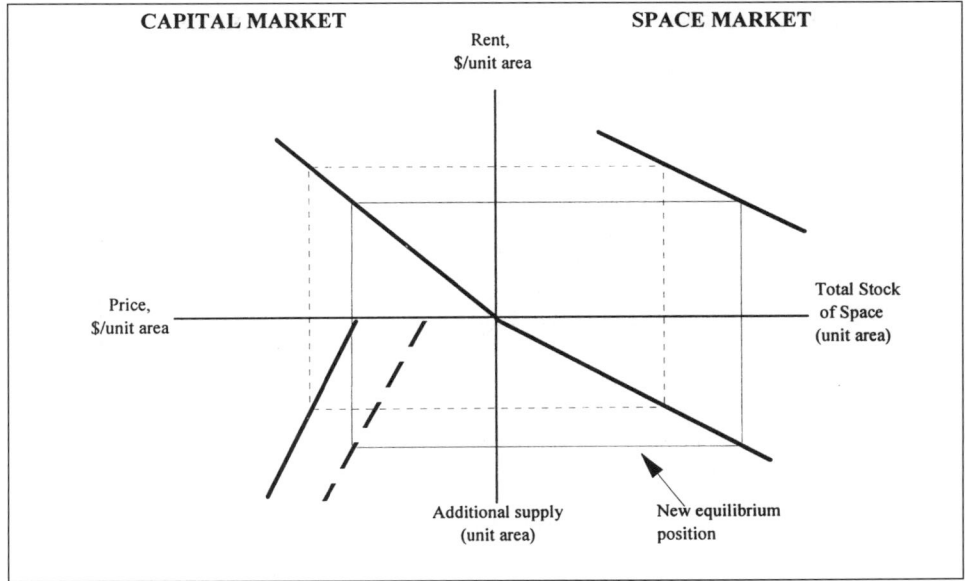

Figure 7.1   A Changed Supply Schedule with Increased Land Supply

cost will likewise increase, but there will also be an increase in the diversity of delivery methods. Lower plot ratios will probably mean that developers will not benefit as much from the economies achieved in high-rise construction as was previously the case. The overall result should be an increase in the slope of the supply curve with a reduced intercept. The resulting equilibrium position following this scenario is presented in Figure 7.2.

Following this scenario into Quadrants 1 and 2 suggests that there should be a substantial decline in rents and prices of real estate in Hong Kong, as could be expected. Much of Hong Kong's wealth is at present invested in real estate, and the outcome of such a scenario would certainly cause public and private concern. There are a large number of additional factors that may have an impact on the analysis presented here, including the development of transportation infrastructure. However, it can also be argued that a continuation of the economic integration of Hong Kong with China will eventually lead to the question of functional and physical integration, and what implications the integration brings to factor supplies.

Effect of the Changing Rules on Presales

The measures taken by the Hong Kong government to slow the real estate market down in mid-1994 could perhaps have been regarded as populist. As it happened

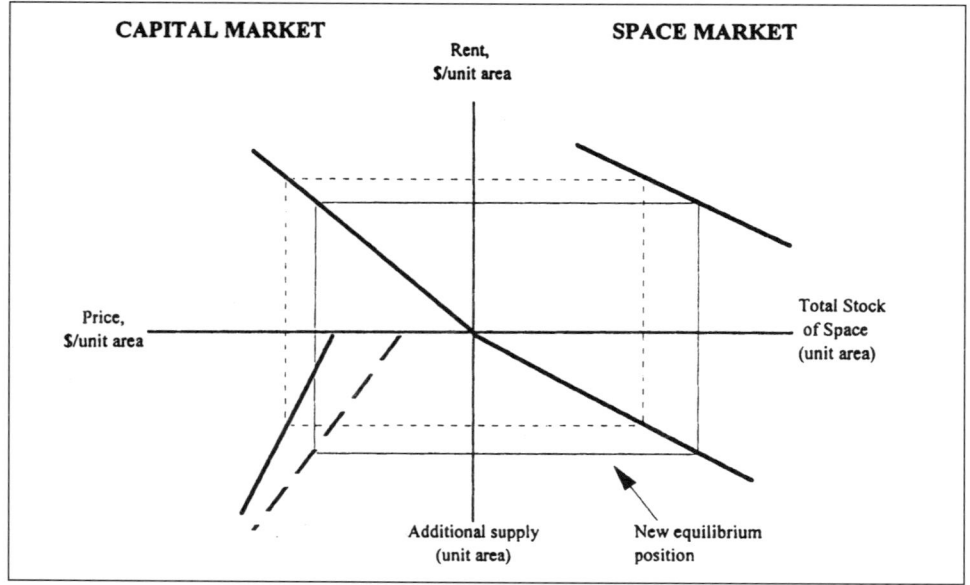

Figure 7.2 Changed Supply Schedule with Increased Land Supply and Lower Density Development

some time ago, at the same time as the market appeared to be slowing down in any event at the time the measures were taken, the analysis presented below presents some evidence about what the eventual outcome of the measures might have been. In particular, we consider what the effect of a curtailment in presales were on the price mechanism. As it turns out, the concern with restricting presales arose again in 1997 as the residential market appeared to be poised for another period of intense speculative activity.

Presales rules were changed in mid-1994 when the government adopted anti-speculation measures to rein in what was perceived to be spiralling increases in real estate prices in Hong Kong. Three policies that had important bearing on the functioning of the presales system in Hong Kong were modified. The first involved a measure that prohibited the resale of uncompleted units bought through presale arrangements. The second is the stipulation that presale arrangements of uncompleted flats be carried out not more than nine months prior to the date of assignment of the sale and purchase agreement.[1] The third involves the change in the rules governing internal sales of newly constructed units. The proportion of flats that could be allocated by internal sales was reduced to 10% from 50%, effectively forcing developers to bear the risk of marketing completed units directly to the public and without the benefit of being able to presell their stock to real estate agents and other investors.

The policy changes introduced in June 1994 had an influence on the demand for asset ownership (Quadrant 2) and on the development market (Quadrant 3). The demand for asset ownership was affected mostly by the provision which banned the resale of uncompleted units. The development market, meanwhile, was affected by all three provisions.

It has been pointed out in Chapter 4 that the presales system affects the demand for asset ownership through lower required purchaser equity which lowers the barrier to entry into the market, as well as the lower barrier to exit due to the absence of provisions banning resale of uncompleted units. The low barrier to entry into the sector is not affected by the policy measures introduced in June 1994. The barrier to exit, however, has been considerably altered. The provision banning resale of uncompleted units is a significant disincentive to purchasers from taking part in aggressive short-term investment strategies in the primary housing market. As the low entry and exit barriers in a sense function together, an increase in the exit barrier causes a still low entry barrier to lose much of its attraction to short-term investors. The ban on resale of presold units, therefore, increased the investment risks in holding housing units. When considered within an investment analysis framework, this would cause an increase in the risk premium which in turn leads to an increase in capitalization rates and to a reduction of prices. This could be represented in a clockwise rotation of the ray in the second quadrant. From an owner-occupier perspective, it would simply exclude those purchasers without the means of reasonably obtaining the required equity to secure the purchase, and would thus eliminate the advantage of the primary market over the secondary market (i.e. lower entry barriers). A reduction in demand could be expected with a consequent decline in prices.

The development sector, meanwhile, is affected by all three policy measures. As discussed in Chapter 5, presales help the developer in two ways. The first is during the development stage by improving cash flow and thus reducing development risk. One could demonstrate that the early realization of funds from presales would reduce borrowing which will in turn reduce development costs. The second is during the marketing stage. The developer can do away with part of the cost of work-in-progress (inventory carrying cost) if the presale arrangement is efficient. An efficient presale system will therefore translate into smaller marginal cost per unit, i.e. a flatter supply curve.

The restriction imposed on developers to carry out presale arrangements only twelve months before occupation effectively means that presales could be carried out only around six months prior to completion, given that there is an ordinary six-month gap between completion and the granting of an occupation permit. The usefulness of the presales system as an alternative source of development finance is therefore considerably weakened.

The two other policies, i.e. limiting the number of units that could be sold through internal arrangements and the ban on resale of presold units considerably increases the risks of developers during the marketing stage. These two measures, incidentally, are closely related. Quite simply, the internal sale arrangement could work only if there is no resale restriction, for the very purpose of the internal sale arrangement is to partly shift the burden of marketing to real estate agents. But the restriction imposed on the resale of uncompleted units have left real estate agents without the ability to resell the units before completion and consequently also losing the ability to select the optimum timing for the sale of these units.

The two latter measures would have an important impact on the inventory management strategies of developers with regard to the units under completion. In particular, it would have limited the choice of developers to reduce their exposure to risks in the real estate market. Under the new arrangement, the developer bears much of the inventory risk simply because the developer has to hold more inventory, and because developers are forced to sell 90% of their newly completed stocks directly to the market. The timing of the release of the developments as well as the pricing of the new units therefore become much more critical factors. These restrictions would act to prevent developers from stabilizing cash flow, and consequently it increases developers' financial risk. It would likewise raise the overall cost of real estate development, and in the long run such costs could result in higher prices for home buyers with all other factors equal.

We can demonstrate the effect of the change of the presales rules on prices and rents: the anti-speculation rules in June 1994 increase unit costs through increased

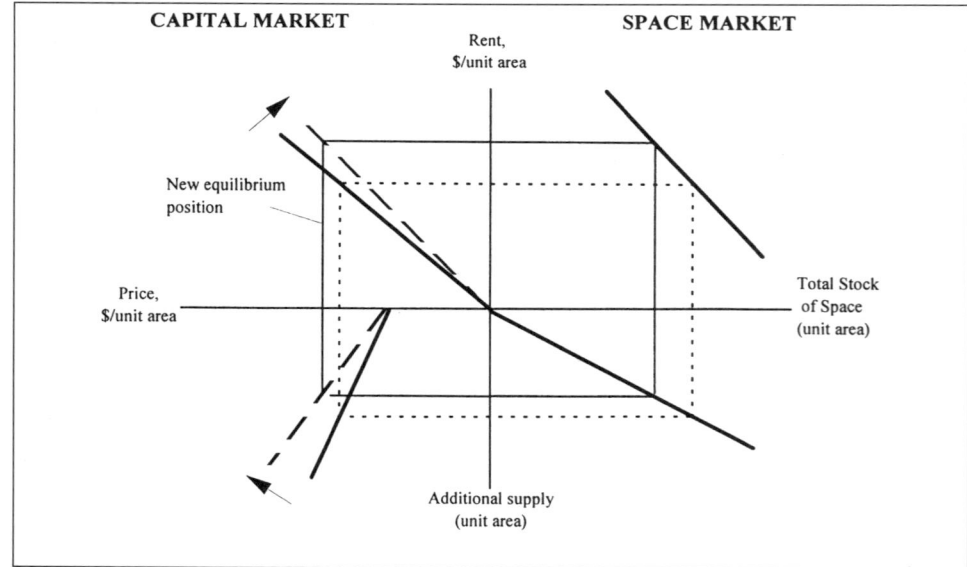

Figure 7.3 Effect of Restrictions on Presales Rules

interest costs and a less efficient sale system, and thus leads to a steeper slope in the supply curve. Following the analysis through the quadrants, the new equilibrium position would be to decrease new supply and increase rent and prices (see Figure 7.3).

Effect of the Proposed Mortgage Corporation

As has been discussed in substantial detail elsewhere (Chau, 1993; Ho and Chau, 1992), the Hong Kong economy's structural adjustment over the last decade and a half towards high value added services activities, and banking and finance in particular, has been dramatic, with some 580 000 employment opportunities created in banking and finance alone since 1987 (Fu, 1996). The importance of Hong Kong's role as regional financial centre, and specifically the role of the financial sector in Hong Kong's continued economic development and employment structure, has attracted attention and policy initiatives to ensure international confidence in the system.

Two phenomena have caused regulatory concern in Hong Kong that are of particular interest for the purpose of this publication. Firstly, the development of real estate credit risk concentration (Chapter 4) to the extent that around 40% of total lending in 1994 was to the real estate sector, has caused regulators to use moral suasion in attempts to reduce (or at least stabilize) the proportion of lending to the real estate sector (HKMA, 1994b). The policy measures that were aimed at curbing speculation in the residential real estate sector in Hong Kong included a recommended limit of 70% in loan to value ratios for bank lending to purchasers of housing units. These measures were perhaps more important as symbolic gesture of regulators' resolve to ensure systemic stability in Hong Kong rather than of any immediate consequence — both for the critical role of the banking sector in the economy and also to pre-empt any additional concerns about systemic stability surrounding the change of sovereignty in 1997.

The second concern revolves around the financial sector's ability to satisfy demand for housing finance to home purchasers over the next decade. Although credit risk concentration is of direct relevance and will be returned to, there are other factors constraining the supply of mortgages to prospective home purchasers. In a recent publication, the HKMA compared aggregate outstanding residential mortgage loans in Hong Kong as a proportion of GDP to similar measures in the US and UK, based on the empirical observation that as per capita GDP has expanded in these countries, so too has the proportion of mortgage debt to GDP (see Figure 7.4) (HKMA, 1996). In 1995, outstanding mortgage debt to GDP was at 22.1% in Hong Kong compared to around 50% in the US and 60% in the UK. Based on the assumption that the outstanding mortgage debt to GDP could follow a similar pathway and reach around

50% in 2005, the HKMA projected that total nominal demand for mortgage finance could reach around HK$1970 billion (HK$871 billion at 1995 prices). The HKMA further assumed that if the financial sector followed the HKMA's own prudential preference for lending to expand in line with nominal GDP growth only, in order not to increase further present levels of credit risk concentration, the potential supply of housing finance would increase to HK$523 billion at 1995 prices (HKMA, 1996). Figure 7.5 presents a graphical summary of this analysis.

It is instructive to point out other concerns about the potential supply of mortgage finance in Hong Kong. In 1994, the HKMA estimated that around 68% of the aggregate mortgage portfolio were for properties of less than ten years old, around 23% for properties of ten to twenty years old, and around 9% for properties more than 20 years old. It was further estimated that the average outstanding contractual life of the portfolio was around fifteen years, with complete prepayment in 1994 around 10% of total outstanding loans by value (HKMA, 1994c). These statistics suggest that the majority of mortgages in the portfolio are fairly new, and thus for properties that were transacted at possibly substantially higher prices than the properties secured by those mortgages approaching maturity.[2] Liquidity released into the financial system through discharging of older mortgages is therefore unlikely to satisfy the demand for new funds as long as credit risk concentration remains a concern and lending is constrained as a consequence.

In all, as long as it is assumed that it is a desirable public policy to facilitate the satisfaction of the maximum possible proportion of home ownership demand in society, there appears to be the development of a systemic constraint in housing finance. On the one hand, the statistics presented above suggest that the supply of mortgage finance from endogenous sources appears to be insufficient to satisfy demand; while on the other hand continued lending to the real estate sector also contradicts the paramount regulatory objective of a stable financial system in Hong Kong. Since 1994 the problems described here have subsided somewhat, with deposits in the financial sector increasing by some 26% in 1995, thus triggering a minor price war between providers of mortgages as pressure to lend surfaces in the banking sector. An improvement in the availability of loanable funds, however, in itself does little to relieve the acute systemic problem of credit risk concentration.

It was pointed out earlier that public policy initiatives since 1991 aimed at ensuring prudent lending were possibly symbolic to emphasize regulatory forbearance (see Chapter 4). To some extent the constraints on supply of mortgage finance were already visible in Hong Kong at that time. In order to manage their own credit risk, banks have acted by increasing the spread of mortgage rates over the Best Lending Rate after 1991 (Figure 4.13), as well as by decreasing loan to valuation (LTV) ratios for new mortgages (Table 4.2). As Fu (1995) points out, this introduced absolute household wealth as a constraint on owner-occupier demand as an immediate consequence, but

Ratio of Mortgage Debt Outstanding to GDP

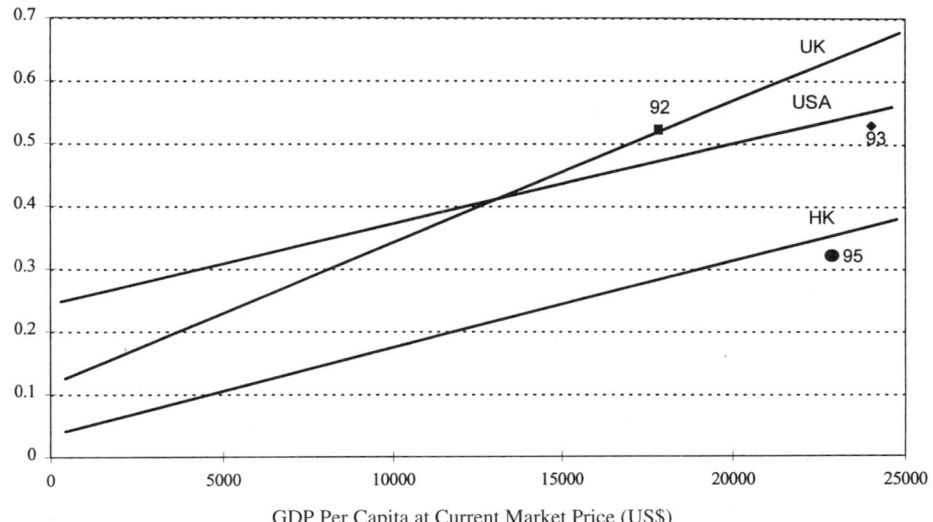

Source: Following Hong Kong Monetary Authority, Mortgage Corporation Proposal, 1996.

Figure 7.4 Mortgage Debt Outstanding and GDP Per Capita (HK, US, UK)

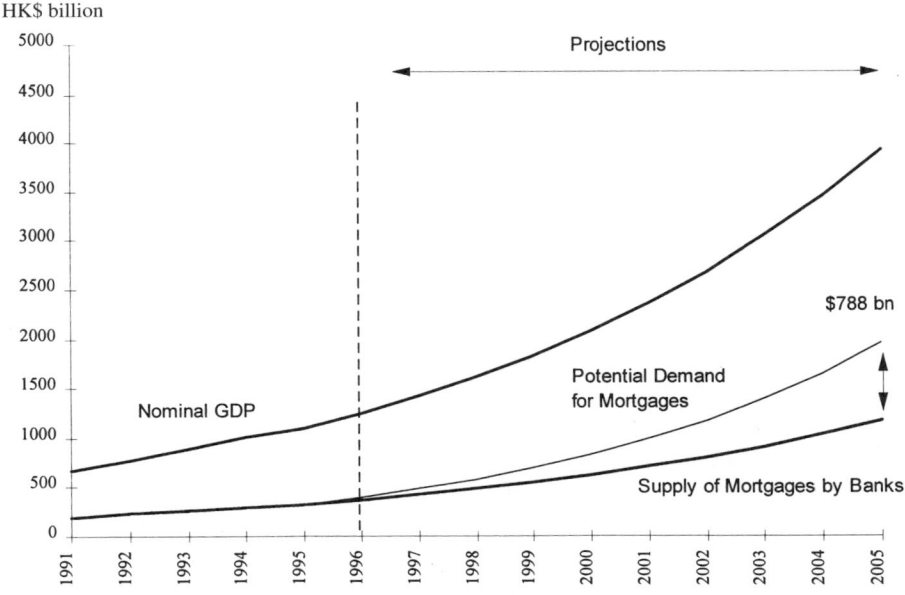

Source: Following Hong Kong Monetary Authority, Mortgage Corporation Proposal, 1996.

Figure 7.5 Potential Demand-Supply Gap in Home Financing

it also introduces the preferred composition in which households choose to hold their wealth portfolio as a constraint. In both cases this suggests a reduction in demand for owner-occupation. Inadvertently, a form of rationing of mortgage finance appears to have been occurring during the period 1991–1994 as real estate credit risk concentrated on the banking sector, and banks attempted to maintain mortgage transaction volume (an important source of bank earnings originate from lending transactions). Increasing mortgage interest rates alone would act to rotate the ray in Quadrant 2 in a clockwise direction, thereby increasing the user cost of housing capital for owner-occupiers and capitalization rates for investors, and so lead to decreasing asset prices and individual household wealth. But the prospect of an illiquid real estate market as a consequence of paralysis in lending demands further policy initiatives despite the fact that this prospect has receded somewhat following increased lending activities in the first half of 1996.

In April 1996 the HKMA released a proposal to create a Hong Kong mortgage corporation (MC) which could relieve the constraints on real estate finance arising from sectoral credit risk concentration in the banking sector on the one hand, while strengthening system-wide capacity to allocate and manage real estate credit risk concentration on the other (HKMA, 1996). Based on the fact that Hong Kong practically does not have a secondary market for mortgage assets, it was proposed to develop a secondary market for mortgages and so create the required liquidity that would allow mortgages to be traded out of the sector where they mostly originate, namely the banking sector. The MC would act as an intermediary in the bond market, and would purchase suitable mortgages from the banking sector as assets for its own portfolio, so providing the banking sector with liquidity for their mortgage assets and the opportunity to originate new mortgages with the funds so liquidated. In turn, it would fund its own operation by one or both of two ways: it would offer its own debt securities in the market and use the proceeds to fund its mortgage purchases from the banking sector; or it could issue securities backed by pools of mortgages originating in the banking sector.

The securities issued by the mortgage corporation are intended to be highly attractive investment instruments with excellent credit ratings offered to institutional investors such as pension funds and insurance companies. This would have the effect of indirectly utilizing these institutions' investment funds flow to finance residential mortgages by transforming mortgages into financial instruments appropriate to the needs of these institutions, namely low-risk, highly liquid investments with an active secondary market. In sum, the HKMA is proposing that Hong Kong creates a secondary mortgage market, and as have been the case in other similar ventures that have been successful (for example, the three US mortgage corporations and Cagamas Berhad in Malaysia as an Asian example), it proposes that the public sector takes the initiative in establishing it through the creation of the MC. The proposal also assumes that an adequate demand exists for high grade investment instruments in the Hong Kong debt markets, which is not entirely defensible despite advances in the development of the Hong Kong bond market over the last few years.

The development of secondary mortgage markets elsewhere have been highly successful as a policy initiative to relieve credit risk concentration in the banking sector, provide liquidity to mortgage originators and develop infrastructure to facilitate better systemic diversification of sectoral credit risk in the financial system. For the purpose of this analysis (and for reasons presented below), we use the FDW model to assess the likely outcome if the initiative to create a mortgage corporation is successful.

As has been pointed out, the development of a mortgage corporation would act to relieve the concentration of mortgages held in the banking sector, by allowing mortgages to be traded as liquid assets to new intermediaries that function in the bond market. We see two immediate effects from the sale of mortgages into a non-bank secondary market. Firstly, there will be an infusion of loanable funds to the banking sector from non-bank and non-depository services, as bank capital previously tied up in mortgages becomes available for relending. This does not imply that relending to the real estate sector is automatic or even desirable, simply that loanable funds become available and that potential real estate borrowers have competitive access to these funds. Secondly, credit risk concentration in the banking sector will be reduced as mortgages are traded out of the banking sector into the non-bank secondary market.

An increase in loanable funds and a decrease in credit risk concentration in the banking sector should have at least two consequences for real estate lending. Firstly, it should function to lower the spread of mortgage rates over the Best Lending Rate, as the risks to banks of further lending to real estate decreases. The outcome of this should be generally lower mortgage rates for new mortgages and lower mortgage repayment instalments for house purchasers. And secondly, the greater availability of funds and the prospect of mortgage liquidity should reduce pressure to maintain mortgage transaction volume through lower LTV ratios, thus resulting in generally higher LTV ratios and accessibility to mortgage finance to a wider range of households through reduced wealth constraints.

If we locate this analysis within the FDW model the introduction of a mortgage corporation should lead to a counter-clockwise rotation of the ray in Quadrant 2 and consequent price increases, as mortgage rates decrease and household demand for housing assets increases. If supply is allowed to adjust freely to price signals, this will result in an increase in new construction and then to an increase in the stock of housing units, and to a decrease in rents if the rental demand levels remains the same (see Figure 7.6). As has been discussed in Chapter 5, however, the Hong Kong real estate market is characterized by significant constraints in land supply. In the case of Hong Kong, therefore, the initial tendency of prices to increase as a result of increased funds flow and reduction in risks in the banking sector possibly will not be met by an increase in new supply. As suggested by Renaud (1989), with constrained supply elasticity the availability of credit could very well act to increase prices further as consumer surplus dictates rationing of available stock. This is shown in Figure 7.7 where there is a kinked supply curve in Quadrant 3. Under these circumstances the introduction of a mortgage corporation could lead to greater increase in price levels if supply cannot adjust sufficiently to meet the price signals.

However, it remains to be pointed out that the introduction of a mortgage corporation has the potential to change aggregate and individual institution risk in the banking sector. Firstly, with the ready availability of a secondary mortgage market, moral hazard increases in the origination of mortgages with the knowledge that these assets may not be held in banks' asset portfolio. Secondly, asset securitization experience in the US and other markets has shown that the most attractive assets for sale into secondary markets are low risk ones, which then become the first assets traded out of originators' portfolios. Both these circumstances have the potential to increase the portfolio risk of mortgages remaining in the banking sector — and thereby also mortgage interest rates. The creation of a secondary mortgage market therefore does not eliminate risks; it simply reallocates risks to different sectors in the financial system.

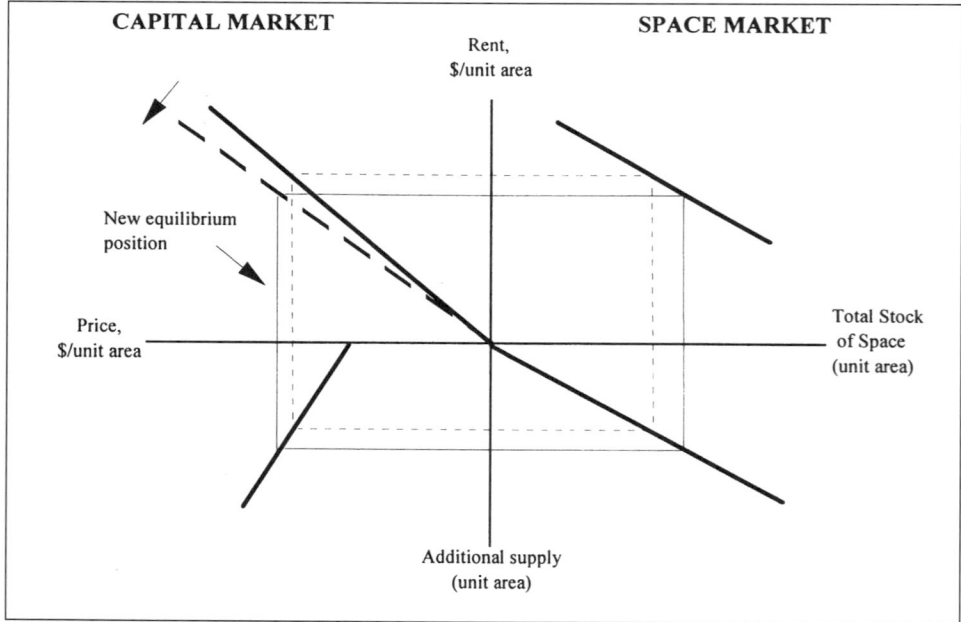

Figure 7.6   The Effect of the Formation of a Mortgage Corporation in Markets with No Supply Constraints

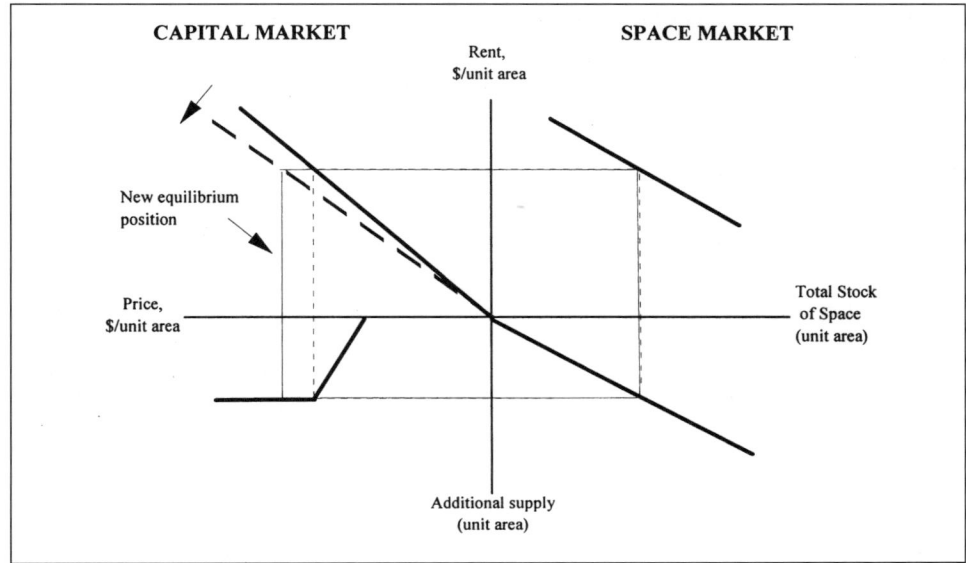

Figure 7.7   The Effect of the Formation of a Mortgage Corporation in Markets with Significant Supply Constraints

This analysis again highlights a fundamental problem that recurs when housing price formation in Hong Kong is considered, namely constraints on supply of new housing. In any long-term analysis no amount of institution building can overcome this most basic constraint.

Concluding Remarks

In this chapter, we have applied the FDW model in the analysis of changes in real estate markets in Hong Kong. The usefulness of the FDW model is evident for policymakers in that the likely impact of alternative policies can be assessed and for market analysts in being able to discern likely impacts of changes in the variables that influence the real estate market. In all three cases presented here the analyses identified restrictions in land supply as a fundamental constraint in the functioning of the residential real estate market in Hong Kong. From these analyses the extreme importance of the challenge to policymakers in the management of Hong Kong's scarce land resources is again highlighted.

However, it is important to point out again that the analyses we have conducted above were mainly for illustration purposes and as such made extensive use of the *ceteris paribus* assumption usually invoked in comparative static analysis. The use of this assumption suggests that resulting equilibrium positions may differ from what transpires, for the actual adjustment process might well involve the interplay of variables which we have ignored in order to illustrate the use of the FDW model.

Notes

1   Given the normal lag between building completion and the assignment of the sale and purchase agreement, this policy effectively translates to six months prior to building completion.
2   Fu (1996) also points out that while the housing price index multiplied 6.8 times between 1984 and 1994, Hong Kong dollar deposits with authorized institutions multiplied 4.7 times, thus making it increasingly difficult for banks to meet the demand for loans. According to Fu, the increasing spread of mortgage rates over the Best Lending Rate over 1990–1994 is a direct consequence of banks 'rationing' available funds.

8 LOOKING AHEAD

The true test of the modern presentation of a real estate economy with the two-sector model is whether it succeeds in going beyond the presentation of the key features of the industry and strengthens our ability to analyse proposed public policy actions. We believe that the robustness of the two-sector model displayed in use allowed this admirably for Hong Kong, while it also allowed us to analyse the essential dynamism of the industry and assess the impact of policy initiatives and structural changes on the sector. We believe that it will be similarly useful in analysing the outcomes of cyclical changes and particular events. The model further allowed us to identify a number of important phenomena that demand further research.

Critical Features of the Residential Real Estate Sector in Hong Kong

This study highlights the remarkable performance of the residential real estate sector in this most open of economies. The flexibility and creativity of Hong Kong's people reflects very well in the response of the real estate development industry's responses to the factors that constrain the delivery mechanisms available to the industry. The biggest factor constraint in real estate development in Hong Kong, namely the supply of new developable land and frictions associated with the redevelopment of well-located but obsolete structures and land uses in attractively located urban areas, has been overcome in the past by substituting capital for land in high-rise, project-scale-intensive developments. The constraints of land supply and more intensive planning regulations in recent years have limited to some extent such technical solutions. Land supply constraints are then demonstrated as being an important cause of rapid housing price increases, with large proportions of existing housing stock functionally and possibly locationally unattractive to many potential purchasers. Policy announcements in early 1997 suggest previous interventions in the market by policymakers that did not consider the distortions caused by land supply are in the process of being corrected, but the lead times will be substantial before the effect of increased supply is experienced in the market.

Credit risk concentration and associated problems with the supply of loanable funds to the real estate sector, possibly the second most serious constraint in the residential real estate market in Hong Kong, could certainly be addressed positively by the creation of a secondary market for mortgages, but the limit to which a Mortgage Corporation could reduce pressures in the financial system is debatable. The resolve of the Hong Kong Monetary Authority in its mission to ensure safe and sound banking in Hong Kong is so important to the future of the Hong Kong economy that it cannot be assumed at all the HKMA will allow the real estate sector to endanger the financial system. It can be expected that there will be continued pressure on the banking sector by the HKMA to moderate lending to real estate.

Conclusion

Substantively, the key features of the Hong Kong real estate industry are remarkably well adapted to its open economy. These institutional, regulatory and financial features should not be dealt with casually if the industry's remarkable flexibility and high efficiency is to be maintained, and Hong Kong is to continue as an important model to study for other societies wishing to learn from it. The Hong Kong real estate industry's organization, structure and performance is a major point of reference given the worldwide trend towards increasing interaction between local real estate markets and global financial markets.

The volume of analysis that had to be marshalled have made this test difficult to keep within accessible space limits and limits to technical analysis. We also acknowledge that variations of the analyses presented here will be needed to deal with Hong Kong's office, commercial, and industrial real estate cycles, but the core model required to understand the industry's dynamics is in place. Using a software metaphor, the FDW model has allowed us to organize an efficient summary page of the Hong Kong real estate economy from which we can later pursue items of further interest through clearly marked hypertext links.

REFERENCES

Barkham, Richard and David Geltner (1995). 'Price Discovery in American and British Real Estate Markets', *Real Estate Economics*, Vol. 3, No.1, Spring.

Bertaud, Alain (1994). 'Land Market, Urban Form, and the Environment', paper presented at the Second Annual World Bank Conference on Environmentally Sustainable Development, Washington D.C., September.

Chang, Chin-Oh and Charles W.R. Ward (1993). 'Forward Pricing and the Housing market: the Presales Housing System in Taiwan', paper presented at the AREUEA International Real Estate Conference, Mystic, Connecticut, USA, 7–8 October, 1993.

Chau, K.W. and A. Walker (1994). 'An Analysis of the Factors Determining Project Level Labour Productivity of Construction Projects in Hong Kong', in *Changing Roles of Contractors in Asia Pacific Rim*, Proceedings of the CIOB (Hong Kong Branch) International Conference, Hong Kong, May 1994.

Chau, K.W. and Lawrence W.C. Lai (1994). 'A Comparison between Growth in Labour Productivity in the Construction Industry and the Economy', *Construction Management and Economics*, Vol. 12, pp. 183–85.

Chau, K.W., D.C.W. Ho and K.C. Wong (1995). 'The Impact of the 1997 Issue on Hong Kong's Real Estate Market', paper presented at the International Real Estate Conference, Stockholm, Sweden.

Chau, L.C. (1993). 'Hong Kong: A Unique Case of Development', World Bank Discussion Papers.

Clapp, John (1993). *Dynamics of Office Markets, Empirical Findings and Research Issues*. AREUEA Monograph Series, No. 1. Washington, D.C.: The Urban Institute Press.

Commissioner of Banking, *Annual Report*, 1994.

DiPasquale, Denise and William C. Wheaton (1992). 'The Markets for Real Estate assets and Space: A Conceptual Framework', *AREUEA Journal*, Vol. 20, No.1, pp. 181–197.

DiPasquale, Denise (1996). *Urban Economics and Real estate markets*. Englewood Cliffs, NJ: Prentice-Hall.

Fallis, George and Lawrence B. Smith (1984). 'Uncontrolled Prices in a Controlled Market: The Case of Rent Controls', *American Economic Review*, March, pp. 193–200.

Fisher, Jeffrey (1992). 1990 AREUEA Presidential address reprinted in *AREUEA Journal*, Vol. 20, No.1 pp. 165–180.

Fu, Yuming (1995). 'Housing Market and Housing Policies' in Stephen Y.L. Cheung and Stephen M.H. Sze (eds.), *The Other Hong Kong Report*. Hong Kong: The Chinese University Press, pp. 261–285.

Fu, Yuming and W.C. Lo (1995). 'Stocks and Real Estate Prices in Hong Kong', paper presented at the International Real Estate Conference, Stockholm, Sweden, July.

Grenadier, Stephen (1995). 'The Persistence of Real Estate Cycles', *Journal of Real estate finance and Economics*, No. 2, pp. 95–119.

Hakfoort, Jacco and Frederik Pretorius (1996). 'Property Markets in South-east Asia', Discussion Papers in Property Research Number 18, City University Business School, May.

Hastings, E.M. and L.H. Li (1996). 'Mainland Chinese Investment in Hong Kong Real Estate', *The Journal of Real Estate Portfolio Management*, Volume 2, No. 1, pp. 75–89.

Hau, T.D. (1992), 'Urban Transport', in H.C.Y. Ho and L.C. Chau (eds.), *The Economic System of Hong Kong*, Asian Research Service, Hong Kong.

Ho, Lok Sang (1992). 'Rent control: Its Rationale and Effects', *Urban Studies*, Vol. 29, No.7, 1183–1190.

Ho, H.C.Y. and L.C. Chau (eds.) (1992). *The Economic System of Hong Kong*, Asian Research Service, Hong Kong.

Hong Kong Monetary Authority (1993). *Monetary Management in Hong Kong*, Seminar Proceedings, October.

Hong Kong Monetary Authority (1994a). *The Practice of Central Banking in Hong Kong*.

Hong Kong Monetary Authority (1994b). Open Letter to Hong Kong Association of Banks.

Hong Kong Monetary Authority (1994c). Survey on Residential Mortgages in Hong Kong, September.

Hong Kong Monetary Authority (1995). *Report of the Informal Group on Secondary Mortgage Market*, June.

Hong Kong Monetary Authority (1996). *Mortgage Corporation Proposal*, April.

Hubert, Franz (1993). 'The Impact of Rent control on Rents in the Free Sector', *Urban Studies*, Vol. 30, No.1, 51–61.

Jao, Y.C. (1993). 'Monetary Management Theory and Practice', in Hong Kong Monetary Authority, *Monetary Management in Hong Kong*.

Krugman, Paul (1993). *The Geography of Trade*. Cambridge, Massachussetts: M.I.T. Press.

Lai, Lawrence Wai-chung (1996). *Zoning and property right: A Hong Kong Case Study*. Hong Kong: Hong Kong University Press.

Lampugnani, Vittorio M. (ed.) (1993). *Hong Kong Architecture: The Aesthetics of Density*. Munich: Prestel Verlag.

Lee, K.S. (1989). 'The Location of Jobs in a Developing Metropolis: Patterns of Growth in Bogota and Cali, Colombia', New York: Oxford University Press.

Malpezzi, Stephen, Larry Ozanne and Thomas G. Thibodeau (1987). 'Microeconomic Estimates of Housing Depreciation', *Land Economics*, November, pp. 372–385.

Miles, David (1994). *Housing Financial Markets and the Wider Economy*. New York: John Wiley and Sons.

The Other Hong Kong Report (annual since 1989, various editors). Hong Kong: The Chinese University Press.

Peng, Ruijue (1993). *Market Behavior under Restrictive Land supply*. Ph.D. dissertation, Cambridge, Massachusetts: M.I.T.

Peng, Ruijue and William Wheaton (1994). 'Effects of Restrictive Land supply on Housing in Hong Kong', *Journal of Housing Research*, Vol. 5, Issue 2, 263–91, Fannie Mae, Washington DC.

Pozdena, R.J. (1988). *The Modern Economics of Housing: A Guide to Theory and Policy*. New York: Quorum Books.

Rating and Valuation Department. *Property Review* (various issues).

Renaud, Bertrand (1997). 'The 1985–1994 Global Real estate cycle', forthcoming in *Journal of Real Estate Literature*.

Rosen, Kenneth T. and Lawrence B. Smith (1983). 'The price adjustment process for Rental Housing and the Natural vacancy rate', *American Economic Review*, September.

Sharpe, W. and G. Alexander (1995). *Investments* (5th edition), Englewood Cliffs, NJ: Prentice-Hall International.

Tse, Yin-Ching Raymond (1994). *Real Estate Economics: Theory and Policy with Reference to Hong Kong, Singapore and Taiwan*. Hong Kong: EIA Publishing Ltd.

Walker, Anthony, Kwong-Wing Chau and Lawrence W. C. Lai (1995). *Hong Kong in China: Real Estate in the Economy*. Hong Kong: A Brooke Hillier Parker Publication.

Walker, Anthony, and Roger Flanagan (1991). *Real estate and Construction in Asia Pacific: Hong Kong, Japan, Singapore*. Oxford: BSP professional Books.

Wong, Richard Y.C. (1993). 'Real Estate and Housing markets in Hong Kong: Issues and Analyses', *HKCER Letters*. Hong Kong Centre for Economic Research, January.

Wong, Richard Y.C. and Samuel Staley (1992). 'Housing and Land', in *The Other Hong Kong Report 1992*. Hong Kong: The Chinese University Press.

Yeh, Anthony Gar-On (1995). 'Planning and Management of Hong Kong's Border', in Joseph Y.S. Chen and Sonny S.H. Lo (eds.), *From Colony to SAR — Hong Kong's Challenges Ahead*. Hong Kong: The Chinese University Press, pp. 261–291.

Young, Allyn (1992). 'A Tale of Two Cities: Factor Accumulation and Technical Change in Hong Kong and Singapore', paper presented at a World Bank Seminar, February 1992.

INDEX

The Territory of
HONG KONG

SHENZHEN SPECIAL ECONOMIC ZONE

Shenzhen

DEEP BAY

Shekou

LANTAU ISLAND

New Airport
under construction

KOWL

Series HM 200CL
Edition 20 1996

km 0   2   4